Confidence and Crowns

Devotions for *A Daughter of the King*

By Tracy Hill

ISBN: 978-0-9976913-3-7

Dedication

To my large, wonderful family and many devoted friends, whom
God has used to mold and make me into the woman I am today.
Thank you for all the love and support you have given me
throughout the years. Whether you know it or not, you mean
the world to me and you have impacted me greatly, in more
ways than I can properly express. I love you all dearly.

Introduction

My hope is that throughout the following pages which are filled with devotions, stories, and Scriptures, you begin to see yourself as God sees you, that you come to understand and believe just how amazing God thinks you are. I earnestly pray that you gain a new confidence as a result of these discoveries. Far too often we listen to the lies of the enemy, the whispers of our peers, or focus on the doubts we have about ourselves. It's time for us to silence the lies, stop worrying about how others perceive us and cease wasting our time seeking to gain their approval—it's God's approval that really counts. We are going to exchange our uncertainties for certainties. We are going to fix our minds on what God says about us, addressing our areas of insecurity by filling them with truth—God's perfect and blessed truth.

So, are you ready? Then let's begin. God says you are loved, forgiven, and brand new. You belong, you matter, you are beautiful, you are strong. You have astounding purpose. You, my dear, are royalty in the Kingdom of God. With all this affirmation coming directly from the heart and mouth of God, you have no reason to be insecure—not today. Not ever.

"I pray that out of His glorious riches He may strengthen you with power through His Spirit in your inner being, so that Christ may dwell in your hearts through faith." Ephesians 3:16-17

Unfolding Confidence

This devotional is a message of unfolding truths meant to soak into your heart and invigorate your soul. Start at the beginning and discover your identity as it comes to life page after page, building on one concept after another. You will begin with the foundation of love and culminate with your position of royalty. I pray that you are blessed and inspired.

Love, Tracy

Psalm 71:5, "For you have been my hope, Sovereign LORD, my confidence since my youth."

True Story

Once upon a time, there was a princess. She was deeply loved and cherished by her Father, the King. His love for her was so fierce that if needed, He would forsake everything dear to Him to protect their relationship. No love on earth would ever equal the love that the Father had for His daughter. The King constantly lavished His endless mercy and grace over her. Nothing she did could ever keep her from His love. Because of His great love, He also desired the best for her, and that entailed offering His guidance in choosing the right path, and when necessitated, His correction in getting her back on track. The princess had a permanent place of belonging in her Father's household, and she mattered greatly to Him. Nothing about her escaped His notice. He was acutely aware of even the tiniest change in her demeanor; His watchful eye caught every glimpse of sadness and each sparkle of joy the princess displayed. He considered her absolutely beautiful.

He had raised her up for great purpose in His Kingdom. He trained her to be strong and courageous in the face of adversity. He filled her with hope, promising her safety and peace within the walls of His Kingdom for all of eternity.

This, my friend, is the true story of your identity as a daughter of the King. It is a portrait of your life as a beloved child of God, and a description of your secure position in Christ.

Psalm 84:3, "Even the sparrow has found a home, and the swallow a nest for herself, where she may have her young—a place near your altar, LORD Almighty, my King and my God."

7

Real Me

When we encounter our Savior and meet with Him privately, it is then that He speaks loving endearments and gentle encouragements, revealing who He has made us to be. After spending time with Jesus, I find that I stand a little taller, hold my head a wee bit higher, walk with a new spring in my step, and face life head-on with the knowledge of my true identity.

In His Presence I find the real *me*.

In His Presence you will find the real *you*.

Psalm 16:11, "You make known to me the path of life; you will fill me with joy in your presence, with eternal pleasures at your right hand."

The Source

I encourage you to read your Bible daily, devour every Word as delicious Bread for your hungry soul. Believe it as your unwavering, unchanging foundation of truth. Let it feed and nourish every empty place in your heart like nothing else so completely can. The Word of God points us to Jesus who is the ultimate source of comfort and satisfaction we so desperately crave.

John 6:35, "Then Jesus declared, 'I am the bread of life. Whoever comes to me will never go hungry, and whoever believes in me will never be thirsty.'"

You are Loved

Love is the fundamental foundation on which all of our confidence and security is built.

Speaking from personal experience, I know that no matter how old we are, no matter how many wrinkles or gray hairs we have, no matter how tough we act, deep inside our hearts there will always be a young, vulnerable girl who longs to be loved and cherished.

From the moment we are born, our heart's deepest longing is to be loved. Love affirms our very worth. It's what keeps our spirit alive; it fills us with hope and spurs us on. Air, food, and water are vital to our survival, but left alone without love and intimate connection we will fail to fully thrive. Knowing that we are loved makes all the difference in the world. Love is our safe landing place when everything else falls apart. I have a wonderful message for you—there is Someone who loves you more than you could ever imagine! You've been on His mind since before you were even born, and He will love you far into eternity. He wants to be the One you think of, the One you turn to, the One who fills you with joy and hope and confidence. He wants to go through life with you. With His loving-kindness, God will keep pursuing you and drawing you into His open arms.

Jeremiah 31:3, "I have loved you with an everlasting love; I have drawn you with loving kindness."

Captured

There is a space in your heart only God can fill, a void and emptiness He alone can satisfy. Come to Him and find the love that your heart longs for.

From the beginning of time you have captured Jesus' heart, and He has set out to capture yours. You are His beloved treasure, and He gave His life to have you as His own. No detail of your precious life is hidden from Him. Jesus knows your past, and He wants to be a part of your present and your future. He has sought you out and desires that you seek Him too. He wants you to find restoration and healing in His capable hands. He desires to be the source of your contentment and for you to find your pleasure in Him. Invite His love into your heart, and He will radically transform your life from the inside out.

Deuteronomy 4:29, "But if from there you will seek the LORD your God, you will find Him if you search for Him with all your heart and all your soul."

He Knows

Jesus knows how your heart aches and longs to be loved. He knows all the ways you have tried to fill your void and have still been left wanting. He knows that the depths of your heart and soul can only be satisfied with the heights of His love.

Far too often we try to quench the thirst of our souls with temporary fixes. We look to different relationships and roles to fill us up, seeking them for our identity, security, and sense of worth. We sometimes turn to pills, drugs, or alcohol as an escape to drown out the thirst, but that only leads to loneliness and isolation. Or, we try to earn love and acceptance through hard work, perfectionism, and being a good girl. Any of these strike a chord with you? None of these attempts are necessary in the arms of our Savior. He says, "Simply come to me. Stop all your striving and find the love and the rest, for which you've been searching. I am the fulfillment of what your soul longs for."

Psalm 42:1, "As the deer pants for streams of water, so my soul pants for you, my God."

Whole Reason

You know, sadly, it is possible to be a Christian and still look for love, acceptance, and completion apart from Christ; we know that our salvation comes from Jesus, but we haven't grasped the love He has for us. Love is the whole reason He came to bring us salvation in the first place.

One disciple of Jesus, named John, understood this love full well. While writing the Gospel that we call "John," he identified all of his fellow disciples by name, but when referring to himself, he simply and confidently named himself as "the disciple whom Jesus loved." Friends, it is time that you and I take on this same frame of mind and believe with unwavering confidence our secure identity in Christ. You are the woman that Jesus loves. I am the woman who Jesus loves.

Let that sink in.

John 3:16, "For God so loved the world that he gave his one and only Son, that whoever believes in him shall not perish but have eternal life."

Everything

No one person can meet all our needs, and no one person was ever meant to. Every individual on this planet comes with their own personal baggage; we're all flawed and imperfect. Only Jesus, God in the flesh, is perfect, and only He can satisfy us completely. Jesus meets us right where we're at and loves us unconditionally. He knows how we are made, what our struggles are, and what we need. We were created to be filled with God's love first and foremost. Once we realize this, we are then able to enjoy other relationships for what they have to offer, taking the pressure off of others to be our *everything.* Only Jesus can be our *everything.* All other relationships are blessed icing on the cake.

Jesus came to fill us with His perfect love, which means our search ends with Him. He calls Himself our Living Water. Just as our bodies thirst for water, so our souls were created to thirst for God. Jesus came from Heaven to Earth to be our *everything.*

Psalm 63:1-8, "You, God, are my God, earnestly I seek you; I thirst for you, my whole being longs for you, in a dry and parched land where there is no water. ² I have seen you in the sanctuary and beheld your power and your glory. ³ Because your love is better than life, my lips will glorify you. ⁴ I will praise you as long as I live, and in your name, I will lift up my hands. ⁵ I will be fully satisfied as with the richest of foods; with singing lips my mouth will praise you. ⁶ On my bed I remember you; I think of you through the watches of the night. [7] Because you are my help, I sing in the shadow of your wings [8] I cling to you; your right hand upholds me."

Pursues

I am constantly awed and amazed at the pursuing love of our Savior. He left the glory of Heaven; He left His Father's side. He put on the flesh of humanity and wore our sins to the cross. He went out of His way to redeem us and gave up everything in pursuit of His love. Jesus came purposefully to save us with a personal relationship in mind. He gave His last breath to pursue us and remarkably considered it His joy.

Hebrews 12:2, "For the joy set before Him He endured the cross, scorning its shame, and sat down at the right hand of the throne of God."

The Gift

If I asked you to think back over your life and reflect on the gifts you have both given and received over the years, I'm sure some favorites, as well as some flops, would spring to mind. Gift giving is one of the greatest (and sometimes hardest) pleasures of life. Anticipation bubbles up within us no matter which end we're on. Even young children appreciate the exchange—a bouquet of wildflowers in a tiny extended hand, smudged finger prints stamped onto paper (otherwise known as artwork), proudly presented with love. Hopefully good presents—both given and received—throughout your life have outweighed the bad. But even if not, I have great consolation for you: God has the perfect gift just for you. God's gift, named Jesus, was born long ago on the first Christmas Day. The motivation for His gift was love, and as believers we get to reflect on that love not only at Christmas, but every single day.

2 Corinthians 9:15, "Thanks be to God for His indescribable gift."

Love Letter

Getting a card or letter in the mail is a rare and special treat! In this age of texting and emails, handwritten notes are becoming a lost art. I do find glimpses of hope for our lonely mailboxes as I sometimes stroll past the colorful card aisles at the market though. I know that I personally need to be more intentional about sending "love" greetings—that is exactly what our written messages are. Whether it be a note, card, or letter, our words on the inside of the folded-up paper are what matter. The paper is just a vehicle to carry our encouragement and congratulations, our sympathy and appreciation. Some people store away and save the cards they receive, regarding them as treasures to keep in a box for future times, to reread and reflect upon.

God has written a letter declaring His love for us. It is called the Bible. The pages of the Bible, from Genesis through Revelation, are filled with the story of God's love and the great lengths He continually goes to in pursuit of our hearts. The promises that accompany His unending love are also found within the covers of this Holy Book. God's love letter has endured through the centuries and is meant to be read daily as a reminder of His love.

I absolutely love Scripture. It is my foundation for Truth in this crazy world. Any time I wrestle with doubts or discouragements, or I forget who I am in Christ Jesus and all the blessings that come along with my relationship with Him, I go back to Scripture for a good reminder of Truth. The Bible helps keep my life on track. I encourage you to read His love letter often for yourself.

Psalm 143:8, "Let the morning bring me word of your unfailing love, for I have put my trust in you. Show me the way I should go, for to you I entrust my life."

Flooded

I grew up knowing that God loved me, and I received Jesus as my Savior when I was twelve. But, I was thirty years old on the day I felt His love actually wash over me. I was at church alone that morning, standing up in the balcony area. There was a guy on stage leading us in worship. He was playing the piano and singing a song all about God's love for us. As I stood there singing along, I felt the Holy Spirit envelop me, and a flood of God's love wash over me. I began silently weeping, tears flowing down my cheeks as I bowed my head. My body shook from the intensity of my sobs. God's love utterly pierced my heart that morning. The love of God has changed my life like nothing else possibly could have.

I pray that God gives you an overwhelming awareness of the love He's washing over you.

Psalm 36:7, "How priceless is your unfailing love, O God! People take refuge in the shadow of your wings."

Simply Profound

If you asked me to pick a favorite song, I'd have to say that I've had many throughout the years. Although I have aged and my tastes have changed, hearing certain songs on the radio always transports me back to a previous time and place. One particular song that I don't hear on the radio but does come to my mind is one that my dear Grandma taught me. I sang it in my youth and then again to my own children. It's actually a love song, profoundly simple and sweet.

It's a song you may likely know: the refrain echoes with child-like confidence, "Yes, Jesus loves me." It goes on to claim, "This I know, for the Bible tells me so."

My dear friend, if the Bible says that Jesus loves us, it most certainly is true. Nothing can ever separate you or me from God's love! Nothing, not ever!

Romans 8:39, "Neither height nor depth, nor anything else in all creation, will be able to separate us from the love of God that is in Christ Jesus our Lord."

Rooted

While Bible study is an essential part of our Christian walk, some people approach it with the purpose of gathering head-knowledge of Biblical details rather than seeking to know God and His love more personally. They miss out on so much of what the Bible offers. You see, letting God's Word penetrate our hearts is life-changing, while just filling our minds with more and more knowledge *about* Him won't have much effect. The knowledge has to pass from our minds and take root in our hearts for it to make any difference. Scripture is meant to point us to God's love which is so enormous, it surpasses all human understanding and is beyond anything we have previously known on earth.

Ephesians 3:17-19, "I pray that you, being rooted and established in love, [18] may have power, together with all the Lord's holy people, to grasp how wide and long and high and deep is the love of Christ, [19] and to know this love that surpasses knowledge—that you may be filled to the measure of all the fullness of God."

I actually pray this prayer for myself and my loved ones, because there is nothing more important in this world than for us to comprehend the magnitude of love that God has for us. And I pray it for you too—that you would be rooted and established in the love of Christ, that you would be unshakable to the core, that you would grasp the all-encompassing measure of His devotion. I pray that above all else, you would personally know His love.

Perfectly

Over the course of our lives each of us has most likely endured the pain of a broken heart at some point. We may have entrusted our heart to the care of someone who was not completely trustworthy. We may have been betrayed, or mistreated. Others may have failed to love us as we need, desire, and deserve. Too often the love we experience falls very short of the love the Bible describes. Scripture tells us that, "true love never fails." This statement sums up the description of God's infallible love. You see, *His* love never fails; it doesn't give up on us, it never abandons, it doesn't depend on our performance or our behavior. *His* love is unconditional. He won't withhold His love for any reason. If we don't feel His love, it's because we are not paying attention, or because we have withdrawn from Him. God's steadfast love never fails! He is the only one capable of loving so perfectly. But with Him as our example and the help of the Holy Spirit we are to strive to follow in His footsteps and love this way too.

1 Corinthians 13:4-8, "Love is patient, love is kind. It does not envy, it does not boast, it is not proud. [5] It does not dishonor others, it is not self-seeking, it is not easily angered, it keeps no record of wrongs. [6] Love does not delight in evil but rejoices with the truth. [7] It always protects, always trusts, always hopes, always perseveres. [8] Love never fails."

Enduring

How committed is God's love? It sticks with us through good times and bad, happy times and sad. It sticks with us when we're messy and downright unlovable. God's love lasts for all eternity. His love endures forever. Let's sing for joy and give thanks for that!

1 Chronicles 16:34, "Give thanks to the LORD, for he is good! His love endures forever."

Found

There is never a reason to hide from Jesus; no reason to stuff our feelings or emotions deep down inside. Jesus wants us to lay it all on the table, after all, there's nothing He doesn't already know. Whatever we're facing, Jesus wants to face it with us. He knows that His love is where our healing begins. In the Presence of His love is where our hearts mend, our spirits soar, and our freedoms abound. There's no need for pretense with Him. Though we were once lost, in His love we are now found.

Psalm 16:11, "You make known to me the path of life; you will fill me with joy in your presence, with eternal pleasures at your right hand."

Pleasing

We don't earn God's love by our behavior, but His generous love inspires us to live a life that pleases Him. While Jesus walked this earth He repeatedly said that if we love Him we will obey His commands and walk as he did. So, what are the commands that Jesus expects us to follow? How exactly did Jesus walk? The answer to both theses questions is quite simply and beautifully summed up in *love*. As disciples of Jesus our life's mission is to love—love God and love all others. If we claim to love Jesus we will seek to live like Him—showing mercy and forgiveness, and sharing the Gospel of salvation, love, hope, and grace wherever we go. The love of Jesus propels us forward to live in confidence; His love also compels us to reach out beyond ourselves.

Go out now and courageously love others in the Name of Jesus, letting them know of His amazing love for them.

1 John 2:5-6, "But if anyone obeys his word, love for God is truly made complete in them. This is how we know we are in him: ⁶ Whoever claims to live in him must live as Jesus did."

You are Forgiven and New

Since the fall of Adam and Eve way back in the Garden of Eden (Genesis 3), every human has been under the curse of sin. Sin is any rebellion against God— any thought or action contrary to the knowledge, nature, and authority of God. Far too often the reality of our sins weighs us down with shame and regret, like a heavy burden on our soul—for the record, God wants to take that burden from us. Other times we may get overly tolerant with ourselves and think, "I'm okay with God because I'm a pretty good person, I don't do bad things, and I try to be nice to others." But if we're truly honest with ourselves, we'll admit our need for a Savior. Jesus says sin begins in our hearts and minds and is then exhibited through our actions and words. Even if our actions aren't so bad, what's going on behind the scenes, inside our heads, can be pretty ugly.

If you took just a snapshot of your life—pick one day, any day you like—would you feel comfortable having every thought exposed? Would you still feel good and nice enough? If I'm honest with myself, I definitely wouldn't. The very thought makes me well aware of my need for Jesus.

We know ourselves better than anyone—anyone, that is, except our Heavenly Father. He knows us inside and out: all our weaknesses, our flaws and faults, all the things we regret and would rather forget. He knows things about us that we don't even recognize about ourselves. He knows it all and loves us in spite of it. God accepts us just as we are but loves us so much that He refuses to leave us that way. He has a much better plan in store for us!

God can and does forgive every sin imaginable once we accept Jesus Christ as our Lord and Savior. He wipes our slate clean, giving us a new identity as His child. I think this calls for a sigh of relief and breath of praise.

"There is now no condemnation for those who are in Christ Jesus." Romans 8:1

Appreciate

Whether you are new to the faith or have heard the message of salvation for years, it is a message that we should never tire of hearing. It is a message with the power to revive our weary spirits and bring life to our dry bones. The Gospel Message (the Good News of Jesus) is something we should continually appreciate and celebrate, and never take for granted.

Psalm 96:2, "Sing to the LORD, praise his name; proclaim his salvation day after day."

Faith Alone

God's Word says, "All have sinned and fall short of the glory of God." (Romans 3:22-26) I hope you notice that you are not alone in your shortcomings! On our own, none of us reach God's glorious and holy standard. We are all in need of a Savior— you and me and everyone! Scripture says it doesn't matter what our backgrounds are, we all need Jesus. God saw the sin that holds the whole world in bondage and provided The Way to set us free from its clutches. Because of His great love for us and by His amazing grace, He sent His Son to die on the cross, to take the punishment that our sin deserves. God has redeemed us, delivered us, and by the blood of Jesus has purchased us back from the shackles of sin and death. His sacrifice—giving His life for ours— makes us right with God. We are *not* made right by our own effort or goodness, but by placing our *faith* in the *grace* that God has *freely* given. Jesus paid the price once and for all. As He hung on the cross, "Jesus said, 'It is finished.' With that, he bowed his head and gave up his spirit." John 19:30

In Jesus your forgiveness is complete!

Beautiful Potential

Even though we know our eternal salvation is secure, we may still encounter moments of doubt and feel that we're beyond all help or hope, and even be ready to give up on ourselves; but God never gives up on us. He has a plan to restore, refresh, and bring new life to us daily. God redeems all of our experiences, even the bad and ugly. He looks at our messy lives and sees beautiful potential in them. There is absolutely nothing in our past or present that God cannot redeem us from, and nothing beyond His power to transform into something good. God's greatest *good* is refining us to resemble His Son. With God, nothing is ever wasted. If we let Him, He will use our circumstances—past and present—to draw us closer to Him, and if we ask Him He will unleash His power into our situation, and His healing into our hearts. What appears hopeless to us has great possibility with God. So, whatever it is that's holding you back, relinquish it over to Him.

Romans 8:28-29, "And we know that in all things God works for the good of those who love him, who have been called according to his purpose. ²⁹ For those God foreknew he also predestined to be conformed to the image of his Son, that he might be the firstborn among many brothers and sisters."

Redeemed

Redeemed: a powerful word full of hope and freedom.

To grasp a deeper understanding of this word I looked up the definition, and according to <u>Webster's Dictionary</u> the meaning is as follows:

1. To buy back: repurchase; to get or win back
2. To free from what distresses or harms: as to free from captivity by payment of ransom; to extricate from or help to overcome something detrimental or harmful
3. To release from blame or debt: clear; to free from the consequences of sin
4. To change for the better: reform repair, restore

This secular definition sure seems like something I'd read in the Bible, and it sounds exactly like the redemption I find in Jesus.

Thank you, Lord, for redeeming me!

Psalm 106:10, "He saved them from the hand of the foe; from the hand of the enemy he redeemed them."

Isaiah 44:22, "I have swept away your offenses like a cloud, your sins like the morning mist.
Return to me, for I have redeemed you."

Soul Cleansing

Have you ever heard the saying, "Confession is good for the soul?" Well, there's actually a lot of truth behind that statement. God's Word strongly encourages us to confess. He asks us to first *confess that Jesus is Lord*, promising that if we do so we will indeed *be saved*. He goes on to encourage us to *confess our sins*, promising to *forgive us our sins and purify us from all unrighteousness* (1 John 1:9). Forgiveness is instantaneous, but purification is an on-going process. If you're anything like me, and since you're human I have a feeling you are, you frequently come face-to-face with the fact that your purification process is not complete. Not long after the glorious sun rises and your feet hit the floor as you get out of bed, you are smacked with the realization that your attitude still needs some serious tweaking, your mind needs cleansing, your mouth need to be washed out. Don't fret, all hope is not lost. God never goes back on His promises—He said He's forgiven us and He has and He does. He promised to purify us and He most certainly will. He knows our fleshly weaknesses and He's not done with us yet. You can confidently come before Him, pour out your heart and confess. Ask Him to help you surrender to the work He's doing inside. Thank Him for His mercy and forgiveness, and His continual soul cleansing.

Romans 10:9-11, "If you declare with your mouth, "Jesus is Lord," and believe in your heart that God raised him from the dead, you will be saved... As Scripture says, "Anyone who believes in him will never be put to shame."

Remember Me

While writing the Bible study, "A Daughter of the King: Gaining Confidence as a Child of God," I came across what is now one of my new favorite verses:

"Psalm 25:7, "Do not remember the sins of my youth and my rebellious ways; according to your love remember me, for you, LORD, are good."

This verse speaks of God's tenderness towards me. When He looks at me He's not preoccupied with my mistakes or sins. He's not replaying them in His mind or aloud to shame me. When He looks at me He sees past it all, with love in His eyes He just sees *me*—His precious daughter, His beloved Sweet Pea.

Priceless Benefits

Being a child of God comes with many priceless benefits—benefits only God can give. His benefits are blessings of miraculous design. I am literally speechless as I read over the benefits He bestows: forgiveness, healing, redemption, renewal, satisfaction, righteousness, justice, compassion, mercy, grace, commitment, and love. All of these and more are yours and mine in the Lord. On top of all the countless blessings that God grants, I hope you know just how far He removes the guilt of your sins—*as far as the east is from the west*. Can't get much further than that.

I'm including this whole section of Scripture for you to meditate on. Let it sink in and comfort your soul. Underline your favorite benefit if you'd like.

Psalm 103:1-12, "Praise the LORD, my soul;

all my inmost being, praise his holy name.

² Praise the LORD, my soul,

and forget not all his benefits—

³ who forgives all your sin and heals all your diseases,

⁴ who redeems your life from the pit

and crowns you with love and compassion,

⁵ who satisfies your desires with good things

so that your youth is renewed like the eagle's.

⁶ The LORD works righteousness
and justice for all the oppressed.
⁷ He made known his ways to Moses,
his deeds to the people of Israel:
⁸ The LORD is compassionate and gracious,
slow to anger, abounding in love.
⁹ He will not always accuse,
nor will he harbor his anger forever;
¹⁰ he does not treat us as our sins deserve
or repay us according to our iniquities.
¹¹ For as high as the heavens are above the earth,
so great is his love for those who fear him;
¹² as far as the east is from the west,
so far has he removed our transgressions from us."

New Self

Ephesians 4:22-24, "You were taught, with regard to your former way of life, to put off your old self, which is being corrupted by its deceitful desires; [23] to be made new in the attitude of your minds; [24] and to put on the new self, created to be like God in true righteousness and holiness."

When I read these verses, I picture the *old self* in something much like a dirty, stinky overcoat, with mud splatters all over, holes in the seams, and buttons hanging by a thread. I envision the new self in a spotless white covering, with the aroma of fresh linen and grace—that's my version. And I do have a bit of Scripture to back it up:

Revelation 19:8, "Fine linen, bright and clean, was given her to wear."

All I know is that if God Himself has given me this glorious covering to wear I don't want to mess it up. If He's cleaned me up and calls me righteous I surely do not want to fall back in the mud of deceitful desires. I am going to do all I can—with His help of course—to stay away from sin and become more and more like Him.

Such Things

New, clean and pure, blameless and sinless—if you have put your faith in the sacrifice of Jesus, then this is exactly how God sees you! And if this is how God sees you, then don't you think it's about time you see yourself this way too?

Many of our poor decisions in life are rooted in insecurities. Just think of all the shame and regret that can be avoided going forward if we make choices based on the confidence we have as a child of God. Although we can't go back and change our past, we *can* stop beating ourselves up over it, accept God's forgiveness, and move forward in confidence! If God says we are forgiven, then it must be true. We have to believe Him; He does not lie!

Even if we believe God, sometimes thoughts of our past sins and mistakes—that have long been forgiven by God—unexpectedly pop into our minds. It's what we do with these thoughts that matters—we can let them run wild in our heads, bringing shame and condemnation; we can let them steal the joy and hope of the forgiveness and freedom we have found in Jesus; or we can turn our thoughts over to God and let Him fill us with the reassuring, reaffirming Truth that we are indeed already forgiven.

Philippians 4:8, "Finally, brothers and sisters, whatever is true, whatever is noble, whatever is right, whatever is pure, whatever is lovely, whatever is admirable—if anything is excellent or praiseworthy—think about such things."

Brand-Spankin'

2 Corinthians 5:17, "Therefore, if anyone is in Christ, the new creation has come: The old has gone, the new is here!"

That's *you*! The old *you* has gone, the new *you* is here to stay! In Christ, you are a brand new, remarkable creation. You have been given a fresh start, with a brand-spankin' new mindset, new purpose, new passions, new pursuit, and new guiltless pleasures. That deserves a grateful, "Amen!"

Whole-Heartedly

Since we've been washed clean we now want to stay that way, and fortunately Scripture gives us a game plan for staying pristine.

Reading our Bible and living whole-heartedly by what it says (not by what our feelings say, what our friends or families say, or what Satan our enemy says) is our sure-fire way to keep from sinning, and this will help us to avoid future regret.

Psalm 119:80, "May I wholeheartedly follow your decrees, that I may not be put to shame."

Unhindered

Scripture describes life as a race, one that every person is entered into upon birth. Once our race begins, we have a choice in how we will run it—unintentionally (meandering aimlessly), carelessly (bumping into everything), distractedly (looking everywhere but ahead), or with deliberate focus, purpose, and goals.

Our race is tremendously impacted by the choices that we make. Placing our faith in Jesus for our salvation, trekking onward with Him daily, and leaving our sin in the dust far behind, are choices we deliberately make during our race. Once we decide to follow Jesus we are saved from the hold of sin and death, and our race takes on a whole new meaning and direction. Although set free, we must intentionally choose to prevent sin in its various forms (not just the big ones that come to mind, but sins like gossip, slander, uncontrolled anger, selfishness, rudeness, criticism, and ungrateful attitudes accompanied by grumbling and complaining) from hindering and entangling us on a daily basis. How do we do this? Not on our own, that's for sure. Only by running the race with Jesus, locking our eyes steadfastly on Him, letting Him lead us onward to victory. He is the pioneer, blazing the trail before us. When I picture my race, Jesus is filling all the roles—He is my trainer, getting me prepared and keeping me well-conditioned physically, spiritually, and mentally; He is on the sidelines cheering me on, saying, "Keep going, you can do it!" He is my partner, running side-by-side with me every step of the way; He is my coach, calling me on toward Himself, the finish line and victory. How well we run our race depends greatly on our coach, our training, our discipline, and our focus. Let's run our race with the goal of hearing Jesus say, "Well done!"

Romans 12:1-3, "Therefore, since we are surrounded by such a great cloud of witnesses, let us throw off everything that hinders and the sin that so easily entangles. And let us run with perseverance the race marked out for us, [2] fixing our eyes on Jesus, the pioneer and perfecter of faith. For the joy set before him he endured the cross, scorning its shame, and sat down at the right hand of the throne of God. [3] Consider him who endured such opposition from sinners, so that you will not grow weary and lose heart."

Good Fight

Don't let anyone steal your precious crown.

Hold it tightly with all your might.

Persevere and keep the faith,

Your glorious reward is worth the fight.

God, Himself, says He is for you, and...

The crown of righteousness is your Christ-given right.

Be strong and encouraged, don't ever give up,

You are priceless in God's sight.

In the face of adversity don't let your crown topple,

But hold your head high.

The fight for the crown of righteousness is a good and holy fight.

2 Timothy 4:7-8, "I have fought the good fight, I have finished the race, I have kept the faith. [8] Now there is in store for me the crown of righteousness, which the Lord, the righteous Judge, will award to me on that day—and not only to me, but also to all who have longed for his appearing."

Pure Joy

Jesus had intentional focus as He lived out His purpose here on Earth. His focus was *joy*. *Joy* was waiting at His finish line.

Hebrews 12:2, "For the joy set before him he endured the cross, scorning its shame, and sat down at the right hand of the throne of God."

What is this unimaginable joy that was set before Jesus? *You* are the joy and *I* am the joy that kept Jesus' focus. The thought of our salvation and a restored relationship with us were on Jesus' mind as He hung on the cross; our forgiveness was His goal, and our redemption was His purpose. Jesus endured the agony of the cross for the *joy* of *us* being with Him for all eternity. Jesus' sacrifice paid to ransom us from our sins, and He considered it a joy to give up His life for our sake. While on the cross, Jesus proclaimed the words, "It is finished" (John 19:30). With His purpose and joy complete, Jesus is now exalted and seated at the right hand of God the Father in the heavenly realms until a future time when He returns for us.

Now the *joy* set before *me*, and the *joy* set before *you* is to die to our self and live for Jesus Christ our Savior, and for His Gospel. No longer living "me-focused," we instead live "Him-focused." *Our joy* is to know Him, obey Him, and to love, praise and glorify Him with everything we have! We are to continue in the same joy that Jesus had on the cross at Calvary and take up our own cross for Him daily. Someday we will see Him face-to-face and we too will be exalted in the Kingdom of Heaven, but until that day, we will joyfully seek to follow and honor Him here on earth.

Secure Grace

Even though we are counted righteous and washed clean of the stain of our sins, we may occasionally and momentarily fall into our old ways and our old habits while on this journey. A word may slip out, we might do something we know we shouldn't have. We may let go of Jesus' hand, get distracted and venture off on our own in the wrong direction for a second. Fortunately, we can never mess up badly enough that God's grace and mercy cannot redeem and forgive us. (Still, let's try hard to not make it a habit.) And our sins will never cause God to withhold or take away His love.

Ephesians 2:8-9, "For it is by grace you have been saved, through faith—and this is not from yourselves, it is the gift of God— 9 not by works, so that no one can boast."

Let me re-emphasize this: we are saved by placing our faith in Jesus Christ, by the grace of God alone. We don't earn His grace by anything good that we do and *we can't lose His grace because of anything bad we do*. It's an unearned gift.

In the security of God's grace, we find a reason for confidence.

The confidence I speak of throughout this devotional is not a worldly, boastful, self-reliant confidence, but a humble, holy, God-reliant one. I thought I would share the Biblical meaning of the word "confidence," which I found on the website Biblestudytools.com:

Confidence*: certainty and assurance of one's relationship with God, a sense of boldness that is dependent on a realization of one's acceptance by God, and a conviction that one's destiny is secure in God.*

The grace of God is so lavishly generous, His grace is not a one-time-deal; His ear is always open to hear our confessions and receive our repentance, He readily offers us new mercies daily. In His grace, there is no fear of losing our salvation. We are forever sealed with His Holy Spirit. This secure grace is the magnificent and indisputable reason for our confidence.

Our Story

Each one of us who has been redeemed by God becomes a poster child of His goodness, love, and power through Jesus Christ. As His children, we each have sin that has been forgiven, we each have a life that's been transformed, and we each have a story to tell—a story that brings glory to God, our Heavenly Father.

Psalm 107:1-2, "Give thanks to the LORD, for he is good; his love endures forever. ² Let the redeemed of the LORD tell their story— those he redeemed from the hand of the foe."

His

I'm calmed by the fields and enthralled by the sea.

In the Creator of these I find my true identity.

I am a child of God, a daughter of the King.

I am blessed beyond measure to say that Jesus is mine and I am His.

On these truths I plant my feet and lift my hands.

I do not fear, for I trust His love and His perfect plans.

Song of Songs 7:10, "I belong to my beloved, and his desire is for me."

You Belong

Far too many of our choices and actions are fueled by the desire to fit in, be accepted, and belong. From a very young age until our last dying breath, our hearts long for a place of significance among others. Unfortunately, this longing can cause us to do some foolish and harmful things; we may even lower our standards, bend our principles, and forget our morals in the pursuit of belonging. An equally sad response is when we withdraw or isolate as a means of self-protection, removing ourselves from any possibility of rejection. Satan, our enemy, loves when we choose either of these responses—the first leaves us open to sin and shame, the second gets us all alone where he can relentlessly prey on us. There is a third response though that our enemy hopes we never choose: It is one of confidence and security in who we really are—a member of God's family—standing firm against his lie that we don't belong.

Knowing we belong to God and His holy family gives us the confidence we need, enabling us to never compromise our integrity just to please others and be accepted by them, and to never again isolate as a means of protection. We have a loving Father who accepts us as we are, who never excludes us, and who desires the best for us.

I've discussed this topic with women before and hurts from as far back as elementary and high school are still fresh in our minds. Based on my previous encounters, I am pretty sure that you may have experienced the feeling that you didn't belong at some point as well. There may be memories of things that you've done to try to *fit in*, or times when you withdrew as a means of self-protection that are flashing through your mind right now. I encourage you to make up your mind to start choosing the third response of standing firm in the confidence that you are a child of God and the knowledge that you have a place of belonging with Jesus. Take your thoughts and feelings of insecurity captive and turn them over to God. Let Him speak His reassuring truth to you.

2 Corinthians 10:5, "We demolish arguments and every pretension that sets itself up against the knowledge of God, and we take captive every thought to make it obedient to Christ."

Created For

We all want to belong in some *way*, and to some *thing*. Families, teams, clubs, cliques, organizations, fraternities, sororities and gangs—these groups give us a place to come together with others who share common interests, purpose, passions and goals. They provide us with a place of belonging, they offer support, and they validate us as a person. It isn't surprising that we seek out these avenues of connection and belonging. God is the One who put this desire in our hearts—He never meant for us to be alone. We have been created for companionship and relationships. Being the good Father that He is, He has provided a warm and loving place for you and me to belong. This place of belonging is open to everyone—it is the Family of God.

Genesis 2:18, "The LORD God said, "It is not good for the man to be alone. I will make a helper suitable for him."

Accepted

The ways of the world are fickle, and its acceptance of us comes and goes depending on our performance, while our unconditional acceptance from God is secure and based on pure love. Contrary to the way we often treat each other and the requirements we impose, God doesn't demand that we are the fastest, smartest, most talented, or most fashionable to be accepted. In fact, He invites us to come as we are. He removes all the ridiculous and unimportant standards we place on each other, and He invites us to come to Him simply *as is*. We are accepted: sweatpants, messy hair, awkwardness, and all. Isn't that refreshing and lovely?

The only thing God does require is that we receive Jesus Christ as our Lord and Savior. Based on His sacrifice alone, we are more than good enough. We are downright extraordinary in His sight!

Romans 15:7, "Accept one another, then, just as Christ accepted you, in order to bring praise to God."

Child of God

In the New Testament (Galatians 3:29) we see that God considers everyone who places their faith in Jesus to be true children of God, "according to the promise."

Isaiah 41:8-10, "But you, Israel, my servant, Jacob, whom I have chosen, you descendants of Abraham my friend, ⁹ I took you from the ends of the earth, from its farthest corners I called you. I said, 'You are my servant; I have chosen you and have not rejected you. ¹⁰ So do not fear, for I am with you; do not be dismayed, for I am your God. I will strengthen you and help you; I will uphold you with my righteous right hand.'"

The word *rejection* may spark feelings of pain. Memories of rejection—from peers, the world around us, from supposed friends, our family, and even those who are expected to love and accept us the most, our parents—may surface in our minds all over again. Rejection can cause pain that makes our hearts physically hurt. If not dealt with, bitterness grows from these wounds. Fortunately, God can heal these injuries and restore peace to our hearts.

Let these words of the Lord sink in and bring healing and restore peace to you: "I called you," "I have chosen you and have not rejected you." Personally, when I read these words I picture myself walking into a room full of people, scanning the scene hoping to find a friendly, welcoming face that would include me at their table. Then as I catch a glimpse of Jesus, His eyes lock on me, a warm smile spreads across His face, and He calls me by name inviting me to sit at *His* table. He erases all my fears of rejection as He calls out, "Hey Tracy, come join me, I've saved a place just for you." Replace my name with yours and imagine Jesus calling out to you, "Hey (your name here)_____, come join me. I've saved a place just for you." Jesus doesn't wait for us to ask if we can join Him, He takes the initiative and invites us to come.

Our Heavenly Father calls out to each of us from wherever we are, even "the ends of the earth." He knows your name and mine, and He calls to us. He beckons us to come. We can come without fear of rejection; we come assuredly knowing that He has chosen us especially. We are His precious children.

Reread the Scripture above and let the words penetrate your heart. The words of affirmation are sure to strengthen your soul.

Deliberate

There is nothing accidental about your place in God's family. He was extremely deliberate in making you His child. Throughout Scripture you will find reminders that you were highly sought after—you were chosen, adopted, and included in Christ. If you think about it, there has probably never been a surprise adoption in all of history. No *whoopsies, how did that happen*? A lot of thought, preparations, and arrangements are required before an adoption becomes official and the baby gets to go home with his new family.

God made His decision and put His plan into motion—He sent His Son, Jesus all the way from Heaven to Earth, where He paid the extravagant adoption fee. All this was done with the purpose of making you His own. You are eternally a part of His family and welcomed into His heavenly home.

Ephesians 1:5-6, "He predestined us for adoption to sonship through Jesus Christ, in accordance with his pleasure and will— 6 to the praise of his glorious grace, which he has freely given us in the One he loves."

To Know

God didn't choose us and save us so we could go on our merry way forgetting about Him. He chose us with the intention of a personal relationship, where we get to know Him intimately, learning His heart, by walking with Him daily. Knowing about God and truly knowing Him are completely different things. The more we know God, the more we know His character which is etched in love. The more we know God, the more we believe in His eternally devout faithfulness. The more we know God, the more we understand His magnificent power and glory. The privilege for which we've been chosen is to *know* the LORD God Almighty.

Isaiah 43:10, "'You are my witnesses,' declares the LORD, 'and my servant whom I have chosen, so that you may know and believe me and understand that I am he. Before me no god was formed, nor will there be one after me.'"

Like No Other

There is a very good reason God is called our Heavenly Father—it's because He is like no other father on earth. There is no comparison; He surpasses them all. Even if your earthly Dad is wonderful, God outshines him too.

If your earthly father is/was absent, find comfort in the fact that that God is ever-present. If your dad is/was emotionally distant, be consoled in knowing that God's love is always there. Your Heavenly Father is approachable and devoted; He is faithful and trustworthy; He is gentle and kind. To straighten out any skewed perceptions of what your Heavenly Father is like open your Bible and read about God's true character on the pages inside.

Deuteronomy 31:8, "The LORD himself goes before you and will be with you; he will never leave you nor forsake you. Do not be afraid; do not be discouraged."

Family Traits

Every family has traits that are unique to it alone. The family of God is no different in that fact, but in many other ways it is very different from every other family on the planet. The character traits of God's family are based on the unchanging morals of His written Word, on His holy values, His unconditional love, and His command to forgive.

He chose us; we now choose Him and His ways daily in return, by living lives of holiness, love, mercy, and grace.

Romans 12:1, "Therefore, I urge you, brothers and sisters, in view of God's mercy, to offer your bodies as a living sacrifice, holy and pleasing to God—this is your true and proper worship."

So Many

Stepping into the family of God is unlike anything you've previously known. There are countless blessings that come from being in His family. First of all, you get siblings—lots and lots of siblings! Now this may bring fear or excitement, depending on how functional or dysfunctional your earthly family is. Regardless, you now have more brothers and sisters than you can count, and by the grace of God alone, you can count *on* them. We receive the blessing of fellowship with brothers and sisters who have the same purpose, passion, and goal as us—to love and glorify God! The whole reason people join groups is to gather with those who share common interests and to have a place of belonging. Well, in the family of God we find this and more—we encounter others devoted to Jesus and to each other. Keep in mind though, we are still just human, each one of us dealing with our own issues, so we need lots of help from the Holy Spirit to preserve the unity that the family of God so deserves.

If you didn't have a big family before, you do now!

2 Corinthians 13:11-14, "Finally, brothers and sisters, rejoice! Strive for full restoration, encourage one another, be of one mind, live in peace. And the God of love and peace will be with you. ¹² Greet one another with a holy kiss. ¹³ All God's people here send their greetings. ¹⁴ May the grace of the Lord Jesus Christ, and the love of God, and the fellowship of the Holy Spirit be with you all."

In Common

The family of God has a commonality which surpasses and covers over all the differences that seek to divide us—His name is Jesus. In Jesus there is no distinction between His family members—not background, heritage, race, gender, status, wealth, style, popularity, or power. We are all equal and one in Christ.

Colossians 3:10-11, "put on the new self, which is being renewed in knowledge in the image of its Creator. [11] Here there is no Gentile or Jew, circumcised or uncircumcised, barbarian, Scythian, slave or free, but Christ is all, and is in all."

Sisters

I know without a doubt every one of you reading this book, and every woman walking this earth desires friendship. We may look around and think we are the only one on the outside looking in— the only one not connected with others in a special way. I have news for you, I have met many women who feel lonely and isolated, and wish for a friend—even though they are part of the body of Christ. Something I have learned over the years is that often women who seem aloof and stand-offish aren't stuck up, they're actually quite shy.

I want to share my story with you as a source of inspiration: When I began attending my current church many years ago, I would quietly slip in and take my seat in the back, and when service was over I would collect my children and go home. Sure, I exchanged greetings with people, but it wasn't until *I made the effort* to connect that I actually started to feel I belonged. When I joined Bible Study I came to know the names and faces of many others in my church. When I signed up to serve in ministry I found others with common interests. I found friends. You may very well be thinking you already do all of this but you still don't feel like you belong. Making friends sometimes takes repeated effort on our part, because unfortunately making friends isn't as easy or instantaneous as it was in kindergarten; it takes time to build trust and relationships. Don't get discouraged, keep reaching out.

Being a friend is a two-way street. It is an equal balance of give and take. It's a partnership. A true friend accepts your silliness, quirkiness, and even your crankiness—and you accept hers. She is kind, thoughtful, and considerate, she gives you a safe place to be open and honest, and share your vulnerable heart. If you want this kind of friend, you must *be* this kind of friend. As much as you need a friend who is a good listener, your friend needs you to be a good listener for them—that sometimes means turning off your mouth and turning on your ears so you can hear what *she* is truly saying. Remember it's a give and take relationship which comes with bountiful benefits.

Years ago, *I prayed for friends,* and along with my effort to engage, God answered my prayers with some amazing women. Meeting with these women every week for the last couple of decades—and counting—along with a hearty dose of God's Word, has been the glue that helps keep my life intact.

If you desire a friend to do life with, I want you to take a moment to pray and ask God to bring a special Christian friend into your life for companionship, fellowship, fun, and support. Friends outside the body are wonderful too, but there is a deeper connection with sisters who share your faith.

Let's pray for friends, and be on the lookout for others who may need a friend and reach out to them. Take my word for it, there are many other women who feel just as vulnerable as you do and would love companionship. It's time for us to reach out and build each other up. In the family of God, we make more than mere friendships, we gain sisters-in-Christ.

Philippians 2:3-4, "Do nothing out of selfish ambition or vain conceit. Rather, in humility value others above yourselves, [4] not looking to your own interests but each of you to the interests of the others."

Clothed

Wouldn't it be amazing if while we all got dressed in the morning, we remembered to clothe ourselves in the same attitude as Christ? What would the world look like if in addition to putting on suits and ties, skirts and blouses, shorts and t-shirts, loafers, heels, and sneakers, aftershave and perfume, hair gel and mousse, we also dressed ourselves in the holy virtues of God's beloved children? What if before we headed out the door we made sure to put on our eye-glasses of compassion, our apron of kindness, our hat of humility, our shoes of gentleness, our belt of patience, and covered it all with our overcoat of love? This kind of outfit would surely stand out and leave a mark in the world. Let's fill our closet with such apparel and jump on board with this bold fashion trend.

Colossians 3:12-14, "Therefore, as God's chosen people, holy and dearly loved, clothe yourselves with compassion, kindness, humility, gentleness and patience. [13] Bear with each other and forgive one another if any of you has a grievance against someone. Forgive as the Lord forgave you. [14] And over all these virtues put on love, which binds them all together in perfect unity."

All-Inclusive

God's family is not exclusive in any way, shape, or form; His family is all-inclusive and has room for everyone who receives and believes in the gift of God. Let's hold out the hope of belonging to a world full of rejection. Gaining confidence in our sense of belonging isn't only for the purpose of making us feel better; with it comes the purpose of including others as well. Remember, the heart of Jesus is all about invitation and inclusion.

Luke 8:1, "After this, Jesus traveled about from one town and village to another, proclaiming the good news of the kingdom of God."

You Matter

God wants you to know that you matter, you are significant, you are seen, and you are heard. If you've ever felt misunderstood, overlooked, or ignored, rest assured God makes it His priority to spend time with you. He can keep the whole world spinning and hold the stars in their place, while still keeping His ears acutely attuned to your voice and His eyes continuously focused on your face. So, lift your gaze to Heaven, speak your prayers aloud; the Holy God of Glory cares very deeply about even the tiniest details of your life.

Matthew 10:29-31, "Are not two sparrows sold for a penny? Yet not one of them will fall to the ground outside your Father's care. ³⁰ And even the very hairs of your head are all numbered. ³¹ So don't be afraid; you are worth more than many sparrows."

He's There

When hot tears are streaming down your face God's own heart breaks for you, and when your belly hurts from laughing God celebrates your joy too. There's nothing He's not aware of; He's concerned with every detail that's a matter of concern to you. Instead of expecting you to carry your troubles all alone, He's there to eagerly help you through. He doesn't force His way into your life, but He is knocking on the door of your heart. Opening your arms to the Lord and inviting Him in for fellowship is an outstanding place to start.

Revelation 3:20, "Here I am! I stand at the door and knock. If anyone hears my voice and opens the door, I will come in and eat with that person, and they with me."

Answered

I myself have cried out to the Lord on different occasions and for a variety of reason. Regardless of how and when my prayers are answered, I know without a doubt that God hears every one of them. He may not answer on my schedule, but I rest assured that His timing is perfect. He may not answer all my prayers with a *yes*, but I can trust that His sovereign answer is always best. While I only see the immediate details of my life in front of me and can only speculate the *what if's* far off in the distance, God knows it all and He doesn't have to guess. My past, present, and future are all laid out before Him. He knows the dangers up ahead of me and where the blessings lie. That's exactly why I choose to entrust my prayers to Him and hope that they are answered according to His perfect will, not mine.

Matthew 6:10, "Your kingdom come, your will be done, on earth as it is in heaven."

Aware

For God's power to be fully realized in our lives we have to recognize that He is there. God's eye is always on us, but are we always mindful of that fact? There is a woman in Scripture whom we can learn a lot from; her name is Hagar. (Her story is found in Genesis 16 and 21.) Hagar faced some serious struggles in her life and as a result she ran away from everything and everyone. She literally left it all behind and escaped to the desert where she suddenly found herself all alone. It was there that God spoke to her, revealing His Presence in her place of isolation. God had been with her all along, but it wasn't until her eyes were opened and the reality took hold that any difference was made in her life. Comforted and empowered by the Presence of her LORD, she was able to go back and face the same challenges she had endured before. Only now she was bolstered with courage, being armed with the knowledge that no matter how things appeared, she was not alone.

God is always with us, but the difference is made when we become aware.

Genesis 16:13, "She gave this name to the LORD who spoke to her: 'You are the God who sees me,' for she said, 'I have now seen the One who sees me.'"

Blessings

I have another lesson to share with you from the life of beautiful Hagar:

Unfortunately, Hagar ran off to the desert a second time, only this time the situation was more desperate because she was accompanied by her young son. Having run out of water in the searing hot wilderness she placed her child under the shade of a bush thinking he would most likely die. She had lost all hope, but then God showed Himself again. He once more made her aware of His Presence and also revealed the blessings she had been missing. Right there in the desert and in her despair, He had provided a well of water to revive their bodies and spirits. She hadn't noticed them before, because she was preoccupied with her problems instead of focusing on The Problem Solver.

Far too often our desperate situations eclipse our view of God Himself and the blessings He has placed in our lives. He has promised that He will never leave us alone. Ask Him to open your eyes to His Presence and to the blessings and provisions that already surround you.

Genesis 21:19, "Then God opened her eyes and she saw a well of water. So she went and filled the skin with water and gave the boy a drink."

Psalm 34:18, "The LORD is close to the brokenhearted and saves those who are crushed in spirit."

Strengthen

There are countless Scriptures encouraging us to pray. We are given consolation that God readily hears and answers prayers. Our prayers are not ever rejected, but instead God graciously views and receives them as pleasing offerings. It is God's pleasure to listen and reach down to meet our needs. He is never *put out* to help us; on the contrary, He is continually on the lookout for those who need some assistance. God knows our human weakness and as His beloved children, He desires to give us His strength.

2 Chronicles 16:9, "For the eyes of the LORD range throughout the earth to strengthen those whose hearts are fully committed to Him."

As Soon As

These are the words the angel spoke to Daniel on God's behalf:

"As soon as you began to pray, a word went out, which I have come to tell you, for you are highly esteemed."

Isn't that incredibly encouraging? While Daniel was still *in the process of praying*, God sent His angel—His messenger Gabriel—in answer to his prayers. While the words of prayer were still on Daniels lips, God had responded with action. God doesn't put our prayers in a stack on His desk, and say He'll get to them later. He doesn't pretend to be listening while His mind is elsewhere. Our prayers matter to God. We matter to God. He is always attentive to our concerns and our needs.

Although Daniel's prayers were answered immediately and dramatically in this instance, we mustn't get discouraged if ours aren't answered in the same exact way. Of course, we'd prefer for God to respond this way every time, but in His sovereignty, He often doesn't. We have to remember that His ways and timing are best, despite what we think or feel. This is where faith and trust come in—we must *believe that God is good*, and that we matter to Him greatly. He sees the past, present, and future, and all the details going on behind the scenes that we don't. So, we have to trust His judgment and His response to our prayers. He might not change our situations the way we'd like, but *He will change our hearts and equip us to face our challenges.*

Even There

If you ever think you've wandered too far from God for Him to hear you, or that your circumstance is beyond hope, think again. There is no place, situation, or sin that is beyond the scope of God's love, mercy, and power. If you ever think you you've gone too far, rest assured He can reach you even there. Yes, from the depths of sin, the distance of rebellion, and the pit of despair, God will hear your cries for help and deliver you from even there.

Jonah 2:1-2, "From inside the fish Jonah prayed to the LORD his God. ² He said: 'In my distress I called to the LORD, and He answered me. From deep in the realm of the dead I called for help, and You listened to my cry.'"

Our Example

Jesus, our perfect example, prayed to the Father, knowing that His prayers were heard. He prayed often—with others, and in solitude. He prayed with thanksgiving in all situations. Jesus knew that when His soul was overwhelmed with sorrow, it was time to pray. He was confident that His Heavenly Father heard His prayers, saw His heart, and had the capability to respond with power.

With Jesus as their example, the disciples knew the importance of prayer, and it was the one thing they asked Him to teach them—how to pray.

Luke 11:1, "One day Jesus was praying in a certain place. When he finished, one of his disciples said to him, 'Lord, teach us to pray, just as John taught his disciples.'"

Jesus introduced them to a new way of prayer, of calling out to their Abba, Father, who is both powerful *and approachable*. He is not far off, uninvolved, and uninterested; on the contrary, our God is very near, very involved, and exceedingly interested in every aspect of our lives. Mark recorded how Jesus prayed before He went to the cross: *"Abba*, Father," He said, "Everything is possible for you." (Mark 14:36) Jesus led as our example of faith and confidence, affirming the absolute Truth that Almighty God is also our Father; He sees, hears, and cares about all our prayers.

Recount

The best way to keep our faith fresh is to reflect on God's nature and recount our blessings every day. As we remember and ponder all of the ways God has previously worked in our lives, our faith deepens in the One who is so faithful to us. When we grow in awareness of all that He's presently doing, we gain confidence for all that He will accomplish in the days to come. Recounting God's character re-confirms our belief in who is He really is. Let's make it a habit to recount what we know to be true—God's holy, loving character; His power, might, and authority over everything in Heaven and on Earth; His faithfulness and endless mercy and grace; His ever-existent Presence; His involvement in our lives and the abundant blessings He bestows. Recounting such truths can't help but boost our faith.

Psalm 105:4-5, "Look to the LORD and his strength; seek his face always. [5] Remember the wonders he has done, his miracles, and the judgments he pronounced . . ."

Three Little Words

Praise, thanksgiving, and prayer: Taken at face value these words are pleasantly simple, but put into action they are life-changing and grand. This classic trio of words is found throughout the Bible. They are expressions we far too often gloss over and think, "Well, that's very nice." They are meant to be more than just nice sounding, they are words to adhere to each moment and to impact every day. When we make them a part of our daily lives something mysterious and powerful begins to happen—our hearts begin to change, and our lives follow suit.

Praise is proclaiming who God is—wonderful, powerful, loving, gracious and kind. Mighty Savior, King of Kings, Lord of Lords. Praise is acknowledging that God reigns from His heavenly throne and that all the earth is His footstool. When we lift our voices in praise, our perspective of God becomes larger-than-life and our daunting worries shrink to a much more manageable size. Praise is the wondrous way to find peace.

Thanksgiving is gratitude for all God has done and all that He's doing. Thank Him for the blessings He continually pours out on your life—the air in your lungs, the sight of your eyes, the grass beneath your feet, the blue sky above. Thank Him for your salvation, and for the unconditional love He continuously gives. Thanksgiving is the marvelous key to unlocking joy.

Prayer is coming before God with the needs of the moment. Carry to Him your burdens, your hopes, and your dreams. Ask Him to mold and conform them to His perfect ways. Ask Him to show you the path He's laid out and the courage to follow in faith wherever He leads. Prayer is the blessed passport to heavenly hope.

As God's precious children, we are invited and encouraged to put these three little words into practice, and then enjoy the miraculous change that occurs deep inside of us.

Philippians 4:6, "Do not be anxious about anything, but in every situation, by prayer and petition, with thanksgiving, present your requests to God."

Continually

Whatever burden weighs on your heart, whatever joy brings a smile to your face, pray about it! God's ears and eyes are attentive to it all. Through prayer and petition lay your concerns before the Lord, and then trust Him with your life and all that's entailed.

1 Thessalonians 5:17, "Pray continually."

You are Beautiful

When you look in the mirror what do you see? Do you behold your beauty or notice your flaws? Far too often we home in on what we perceive is wrong, being harsh and critical, picking ourselves apart, wishing we were different. It's such a shame we don't readily see what God sees. He sees absolute beauty in His precious child. If only we could see ourselves just as He sees us (and most likely as others see us too). Fortunately, with His help in altering our perspective I think we can. We can begin to see ourselves through the lens of love and grace, and to appreciate the marvelous way that God saw fit to make us.

Ask Him to give you His viewpoint on You.

Song of Songs 4:7, "You are altogether beautiful, my darling; there is no flaw in you."

Unique

Why would you want to be like someone else, when you can be uniquely YOU? Our world—not to mention the heavens—is filled with awe-inspiring beauty; everywhere we look something dazzling catches our eye. It's not the things that blend in that grab our attention, it's the objects that stand out. This same principle applies to people too. If we all looked alike life would be so bland. God has made you to be especially YOU for a reason, to add to the beautiful tapestry of His creation. You add a dimension to this world that would be greatly missed if you were like someone else. God created you inside and out exactly the way He intended—He gave you characteristics unique only to you. He formed your traits, qualities, personality, talents, gifts, appearance, and even threw in a few quirks to make the remarkable and complete package of YOU. And I'm so glad He did!

Song of Songs 6:9, "But my dove, my perfect one, is unique, the only daughter of her mother, the favorite of the one who bore her."

Masterpiece

Even in the simplest of creations, we find great complexity. God is the Ultimate Artist, paying close attention to the intricate and delicate details of His work. From mere observation, we may not notice the minute distinctions of His creation, but upon closer investigation we find that each one is exceptionally unique. Let me explain: If we took a trip to the zoo, we might see giraffes or zebras which, from our vantage point safely behind the fence, appear to look alike. All the giraffes are tall, with long necks, long legs, and brown spots covering their bodies. Did you know that the spots of each giraffe are unrepeated? No two are alike in all of creation. The same is true of the zebra's stripes—no two zebras have the same exact pattern. Have you ever caught a snowflake on your tongue? Out of all the countless tiny white flakes that fall from the sky, not one is identical to another. God used the same creativity when He made you. There is only one of you. Your fingerprints are exclusive to you alone, different from every other person who has ever lived. God doesn't make cookie-cutter creations. Something is highly valued because it is rare. Consider a beautiful portrait hanging on the walls of a museum; it is counted priceless because it is a one-of-a-kind masterpiece. All reproductions of the original pale in comparison. The rarity and originality of the artist's work is what constitutes its value. God has a reason for making you exactly the way you are. You are uniquely created by Him. You are a priceless masterpiece!

Psalm 104:24, "How many are your works, LORD! In wisdom you made them all; the earth is full of your creatures."

Wonderfully Made

Psalm 139:13-16, "For you created my inmost being;
you knit me together in my mother's womb.
¹⁴ I praise you because I am fearfully and wonderfully
made; your works are wonderful, I know that full well.
¹⁵ My frame was not hidden from you when I was
made in the secret place, when I was woven together in
the depths of the earth. ¹⁶ Your eyes saw my unformed
body; all the days ordained for me were written in your
book before one of them came to be."

These Scriptures make it clear that you are no accident. God planned on you long before your arrival, and even before the world began. Before the technology of modern ultrasound gave insight to the eyes of the doctor and parents, your Heavenly Father had His eyes on you. Not only was He watching over you, but His mighty hands were lovingly at work, knitting and weaving every bit of you together. God was intimately involved in the making of you! Not one detail was overlooked. All of God's creations are wonderful and that most definitely includes you! It's time you took that to heart and believed it full well. Xoxo

Grow

As a child you may have heard the expression, "Oh, she'll grow into it." The "it" being referred to may have been your prominent nose, your large ears, your long lanky legs, big feet, or few extra pounds. The years may have passed and you find that you still look the same. Sometimes we do physically grow to fit into the "it" that was out of proportion on our child-sized frame, and other times we don't. And that's okay. It may be that our appreciation and acceptance of ourselves as a beautiful creation, just the way we are, is what really needs to grow. Ask God to help you emotionally grow into celebrating who you are.

Song of Songs 1:15, "How beautiful you are, my darling! Oh, how beautiful!"

Celebrate

Take a look around you—you'll notice that at first glance we all appear similar, but look a little closer and you'll notice distinctions in our features. Yes, we all have a nose, a mouth, eyes, ears, eyebrows, cheeks, and a forehead, but within these standard features there is great variety. We all have the same pieces but God put them together differently and made you and me. I am so glad He did! It would be so boring if all the people in my life were made from the same template. God breaks the mold with each new creation, never duplicating a previous work of wonder.

Each precious individual in my life has something special and different to offer. They all add a new dimension to me. And my life gets to add a new element (sometimes surprising) to them. Let's celebrate and be grateful for each other, and give thanks to our creative Lord.

1 John 4:11, "Dear friends, since God so loved us, we also ought to love one another."

Makeover

Have you ever seen a woman literally glow because of her relationship with Jesus?

The more time we spend in the Presence of Jesus, the more it shows on our face. Our countenance changes to reflect His sweet grace at work in us. Others even notice the change in our eyes— ones that before were weary are filled with hope and sparkle with joy. The time we spend with Jesus is better than a day at the spa. He does more for our beauty than any treatments can. He is the One who softens the lines of our face, unfurrows our brow, removes our scowl, replacing them with a glimmer in our eyes, a rosiness to our cheeks, and an upward curve at the edges of our mouths. Jesus is the Master at complete make-overs—both inside and out. As we spend time with Him the unfading beauty of kindness, goodness, and gentleness can't help but manifest on our face.

Proverbs 31:30, "Charm is deceptive, and beauty is fleeting; but a woman who fears the LORD is to be praised."

Inside

Magazines, television commercials, and social media push their impossible, touched up, ideal of beauty on us. Unfortunately, media sets the bar and far too often we try to jump over it. That's exhausting and unfulfilling too. True beauty does NOT come in a "one size, one shape, or one color fits all." Just open your eyes and that quickly becomes apparent, exposing the nonsense of the notion of it all. Real beauty is so much more than meets the eye. Real beauty goes beyond skin deep.

To expand on my point, consider these questions:

Have you noticed how your impression of the most physically gorgeous woman instantly changes the second she opens her mouth in anger, rudeness, or sarcasm? Have you ever witnessed a woman with a plainer appearance transform into a beauty right before your eyes, just because she exhibited kindness and gentleness and her words were seasoned with grace?

I hope you embrace the perspective, that true and lasting beauty radiates from the inside.

1 Peter 3:3, "Your beauty should not come from outward adornment, such as elaborate hairstyles and the wearing of gold jewelry or fine clothes. 4 Rather, it should be that of your inner self, the unfading beauty of a gentle and quiet spirit, which is of great worth in God's sight."

P.S. Scripture is not saying we can't put any effort into our appearance, or that wearing a cute outfit or necklace is bad. It's just warning us to get our priorities straight, by being more concerned with the things that make us beautiful from the inside out. Our attitude and character do more to affect our beauty than any make-up possibly could.

When you're getting dressed in the morning be sure to add some kindness and a smile—they're actually your best accessories.

Flipped

The Word of God flips the world's understanding of beauty completely upside-down. The world tries to convince us that beauty is found *only* in youth, glamour, and its idea of perfection. We're wrongly told that beauty should be flaunted—on obvious display for all the world to see, with overly-revealing clothing—as a means of attracting attention. Instead, God tells us that beauty, value, dignity, and worth are found in every life, no matter the stage or age, shape or size. It is found in our attitude, and we don't have to fight the aging process, but instead embrace it. Gray hair is a symbol of beauty, a symbol of wisdom. Wrinkles are, quite simply, glorious lines etched into faces from both sorrow and joy, telling the story of a life well-lived. God finds beauty in a *quiet and gentle spirit*, in *modesty*, in *wisdom*, in *righteousness*, in *kindness and compassion*. Ask God to give you His perspective and throw off the pressure and lies. God's kind of beauty stands the test of time; it isn't a passing fad or outrageous fashion that comes and goes out of style at a moment's notice.

1 Timothy 2:9-10, "I also want the women to dress modestly, with decency and propriety, adorning themselves, not with elaborate hairstyles or gold or pearls or expensive clothes, ¹⁰ but with good deeds, appropriate for women who profess to worship God."

Yourself

In Matthew 22:37-38, Jesus was asked which were the greatest commands for us to follow, and "*Jesus replied: 'Love the Lord your God with all your heart and with all your soul and with all your mind.* [38] *This is the first and greatest commandment.* [39] *And the second is like it: Love your neighbor as yourself.'*"

In most commentaries and sermons, the *love for God* and *for our neighbor* are highlighted in this exchange, and with good reason—these are the commands that Jesus has given us to follow, and from which all godly living will flow. But I have found there to be an often overlooked, underlying theme: Jesus said we are to love our neighbors *as ourselves*, which brings with it the assumption that we actually *love ourselves*. I think it's sometimes easier for us to appreciate and love others, than it is to even tolerate ourselves. We look at others and think, she's so pretty, so kind, so talented, so organized...and so on. Do we ever apply these gracious, generous thoughts to ourselves? It's about time we start showing ourselves some grace, and begin seeing *ourselves* as special, instead of being our own worst critic. From now on let's determine to conquer our negative self-image, raise our low self-esteem, replace our negative self-talk, stop being overly self-conscious, and cease trying to be someone else!

Let's make a clean break from focusing on our flaws and imperfections, and just appreciate who and how God has made us each to be—*a daughter of the King.*

A Temple

The act of loving and appreciating ourselves as God's lovely creation means that we also respect and take care of ourselves as His creation. Instead of being self-conscious, we are going to be self-aware—aware of how to optimally take care of this body God has blessed us with. We want to bring out the best in what we've been given, by feeding our bodies nutritious food, being active, getting proper rest, meditating on the Word of God, and by taking the time to take care of ourselves—and not feel guilty.

Don't obsess over your looks and body image, but also don't neglect or take yourself for granted. Love and care for yourself—in this way you will honor God. Refrain from things that are harmful, and instead take time to nourish your body, mind, and spirit with things that are beneficial and pleasing to God.

1 Corinthians 6:19-20, "Do you not know that your bodies are temples of the Holy Spirit, who is in you, whom you have received from God? You are not your own; you were bought at a price. Therefore, honor God with your bodies."

You Have Purpose

The all-encompassing purpose of a *daughter of the King* is to love, serve, and honor God, and in the process love, bless, and impact those around her. Living for God is a daughter's ultimate act of worship, and words can't begin to describe the overwhelming satisfaction that floods her soul when she discovers and begins to live out her purpose for God. Psst, you are that daughter.

Proverbs 20:5, "The purposes of a person's heart are deep waters, but one who has insight draws them out."

Qualified

This over-arching purpose of knowing, loving, and serving God will exhibit itself differently in each of our lives. Just because your friend's life and ministry look different from yours, doesn't mean yours is wrong. It very well means you're both right where God wants each of you! Don't fall into the trap of comparing yourself with others, just keep your eyes on Jesus and ask Him to show you the plans He has made especially for you.

Far too many women doubt themselves—they feel unqualified, unneeded, and unable to measure up. This is just not true! It's a horrible lie of the enemy meant to keep us from reaching our God-given potential and having any Kingdom impact. Each of us is an asset in God's eyes, and uniquely qualified with our talents and spiritual gifts to do something incredibly worthwhile. Anyway, God doesn't expect us to fulfill His purpose on our own; He plans to work in us and through us to bring about His good works. He is the one who calls us and equips us for the jobs, tasks, and ministries before us—and Satan cannot stand in His way.

Jesus Himself is the One who qualifies us. So rest assured, you are superbly qualified! Thank Him by joyfully praising His name!

1 Corinthians 1:27-29, "But God chose the foolish things of the world to shame the wise; God chose the weak things of the world to shame the strong. 28 God chose the lowly things of this world and the despised things—and the things that are not—to nullify the things that are, 29 so that no one may boast before him."

Unwrapped

Many new encounters begin, "So nice to meet you. What do you *do*?" ("Do," usually referring to our job.) What we *do* does reveal a bit about us, but it's only the tip of the iceberg. There is exceedingly more to what truly makes up who we *are*. Our identity, value, and worth are found in something much deeper and more fundamental—being a child of God. That is who we *are*, and what we *do* flows naturally from that foundation. God has given His children the desire and ability to do good things. With our identity as a springboard, He uses our experiences, our education, our passions, our sphere of influence, our talents, and our spiritual gifts to impact the world around us. God wraps who we *are* and what we *do* into one beautiful package just waiting to be unwrapped.

Ephesians 2:10, "For we are God's handiwork, created in Christ Jesus to do good works, which God prepared in advance for us to do."

Experiences

Your life is filled with experiences that have helped form you into the person you've become. The good, the bad, and everything in-between. God takes all of it and uses it to move you forward with purpose. With God, nothing is ever wasted. Your background and experiences mold and shape your heart, your sensitivities, and your goals, and they motivate your responses and actions.

Your life's history can help you relate to others on a deeper level. Many ministries are started as a result of someone's personal familiarity—*been there, done that, lived through it, now let me help you*. The testimonies with the biggest impact are those that resemble your own story. Your own experiences can be used to grow compassion in you, and then be used to encourage others who are on the same journey.

Difficult firsthand experiences: loss, grief, divorce, abuse, addiction, etc... Satan would love for these negative hardships to hold you in bondage, away from the abundant life that God has in store for you, and also keep you from making a positive impact in the world. The enemy intends to harm you and render you ineffective by your trials, but God will use these for His greater purpose, if you let Him.

Don't let Satan win by allowing him to keep his hold over you—your personal experiences can be used for good, if you surrender them to God's sovereign care. Let God use your experiences to speak healing, life, encouragement, hope, and joy into the lives of others. By doing so, you will find miraculous blessings for yourself.

Romans 8:28-29, "And we know that in all things God works for the good of those who love him, who have been called according to his purpose. For those God foreknew he also predestined to be conformed to the image of his Son, that he might be the firstborn among many brothers and sisters."

2 Corinthians 1:3-4, "Praise be to the God and Father of our Lord Jesus Christ, the Father of compassion and the God of all comfort, [4] who comforts us in all our troubles, so that we can comfort those in any trouble with the comfort we ourselves receive from God."

Education

In our culture, the official course of education begins the first day of Kindergarten and continues through to High School graduation. Some children begin their education a year or two earlier in Preschool, and others as adults, continue their education after High school onto college and graduate school. Some forego the traditional route and—like myself—go onto a trade school. This has become the *general* standard, but not everyone falls into this category. Some of the wisest people I've known never made it past elementary school or middle school in their formal education. You see, not all education occurs within the walls of the classroom. Much of our learning occurs elsewhere—our experiences, our conversations, our observations, travel, the news, books, T.V., magazines, the internet, and most importantly, the Bible. These various forms of learning are crafted into a well-rounded education, informing the way we think, live, and view the world. Don't let a diploma or certificate—or lack thereof—dictate your worth or purpose. God can use your eclectic education—after He filters it through His Word—to teach, lead, and inform others.

Proverbs 24:3-4, "By wisdom a house is built, and through understanding it is established; [4] through knowledge its rooms are filled with rare and beautiful treasures."

Ultimate wisdom and knowledge for living are found in the living Word of God. Pass it on...

Desires

Don't let insecurity stop you from pursuing the passions God has put into your heart. Refuse to listen to any voice that says, "That's a stupid idea." It was my desire—put there by God—to write books. It's not something I'm especially qualified to do, but I followed my heart's leading. If something is pressing on your heart I encourage you to check it out, see where it leads, and follow it through. You may be pleasantly surprised at the outcome! Your responsibility is to act in faith and obedience to whatever God places on your hearts and calls you to, and then trust Him with the results.

Psalm 37:4, "Take delight in the LORD, and he will give you the desires of your heart."

Sphere of Influence

Home, work, school, your neighborhood, the grocery store. You have a purpose right where you are. Reach out your arms and at the end of your fingertips you will find your sphere of influence. You don't have to travel to the ends of the earth to make a difference—unless of course you are called to. You can make an impact right where you are! The people right around you need you in their life. Make yourself available, then be obedient to the Lord's promptings.

Esther 4:14, "For if you remain silent at this time, relief and deliverance for the Jews will arise from another place, but you and your father's family will perish. And who knows but that you have come to your royal position for such a time as this?"

Queen Esther began her life as an ordinary Jewish girl, but God raised her up to the position of queen, giving her access to influence the decisions of her husband, King Xerxes. As a result, she saved the Jews who were living in captivity under Persian Rule, from imminent annihilation. She had great impact in her everyday sphere of influence. You can too. You are capable of making a difference in the lives of your family, friends, co-workers, neighbors, ministry partners, and even in the lives of complete strangers that you encounter. Take a look at the lives you already touch on a regular basis and there you will find your purpose. Impact them with the love of Jesus.

Skills and Talents

Do you have a special flair, knack, or ability for certain things? Do you have a mind for numbers, a natural way with words, an ability for organization, a keen eye for décor, an aptitude for language, a talent for musical instruments, art, singing, or dancing, or are you a whiz in the kitchen? God has placed within each of us some natural abilities—certain skills and talents that come more easily—that He wants to incorporate into our purpose. Is there something you enjoy doing, something that comes naturally for you, or something you're particularly interested in? I encourage you to think outside the box. Whatever popped in your mind, I say pursue it! There is a use for every skill and talent you have inside of you; it just might be waiting to be discovered. If you want to strengthen your ability, talents, or skill sets with some formal training, go for it! Enroll in a class, take lessons online, expand your horizons, and foster the growth of the skills and talents that God has already bestowed on you. Have confidence in the ability He has given you! Then go on to use your God-given skills and talents to bless others.

Exodus 31:3, "and I have filled him with the Spirit of God, with wisdom, with understanding, with knowledge and with all kinds of skills"

Ever-Changing

You never reach a point when you are no longer useful, or cease to have purpose. Your purpose may evolve, but it never ends.

My over-all, and constant purpose on this earth is to love and glorify God, but beyond that God has also given me other purposes along the way. These other purposes have grown and changed over the course of my life thus far, and no doubt will continue to do so. I have devoted a large portion of my life to my marriage and to raising our two wonderful sons. I spent many years wiping noses, reading bedtime stories, singing lullabies, watching shows with big purple dinosaurs and little blue dogs, driving carpool, cheering at sporting events, all culminating with the wiping of my own tears of overwhelming pride as each of my sons walked down the aisle and received their High School diploma. Anticipating their graduation days would occasionally fill me with dread, as I wondered, "What will my purpose be now?" With them leaving the nest and living far from home, what would I do? The fear and doubt that I was losing my purpose began to creep in. I turned these thoughts over to God and He showed me that I hadn't lost my purpose, it was just changing a bit. He was right, I still have a LOT of purpose in me. Coming out of the other side of doubt, I can confidently tell you that *you never lose your purpose*. You too, have a LOT of purpose in you!

Proverbs 19:21, "Many are the plans in a person's heart, but it is the LORD's purpose that prevails.

Spiritual Gifts

Each of us is born with a tendency towards certain skills and talents that can be grown and developed in us through training. Scripture tells us that we are re-born the moment we receive Jesus as our Savior, and in that very instant we are blessed with the Holy Spirit—God's Spirit—coming to dwell inside of us, sealing us as God's child. When the Holy Spirit comes to take up residence in our lives He comes bearing gifts—spiritual Gifts. These are gifts that we cannot earn, and ones that we cannot learn. They are given to us by the grace of God to help us fulfill our God-given purpose in the church. Everyone who knows Jesus as Savior has been blessed with Spiritual gifts—that includes *you*!

Resist the temptation to look around and compare your gifts with others. There is a wide variety of gifts and for the benefit of the body, God purposefully divvies them up differently. If everyone received the same gifts, the body would be a ridiculously lopsided mess. Each gift is vital to the body and equally important. The following Scripture uses the word "different" three times in reference to gifts, service, and working (exhibition), but all of these differences are united in the same Spirit, Lord, and God.

1 Corinthians 12:4-6, "There are different kinds of gifts, but the same Spirit distributes them. ⁵ There are different kinds of service, but the same Lord. ⁶ There are different kinds of working, but in all of them and in everyone it is the same God at work."

In "Love"

The purpose of each gift is exactly the same: unite, strengthen, and build up the church, and point everyone to the glory of God by showing His love.

Scripture gives us a description of the gifts that God gives. They are as varied and necessary as the parts of the human body. There are gifts of pastoring/shepherding, mercy, giving, administration, leadership, service, apostleship, evangelism, exhortation, healing, discernment, knowledge, wisdom, speaking in tongues, interpreting tongues, teaching, prophecy, miracles, and last but definitely not least the gift of faith.

Let me describe as best I can what a spiritual gift is like: although each one of us should be filled and overflowing with mercy and faith, living with godly wisdom, knowledge and discernment, certain members of the body are assigned one or more of these as their specialty. This is the area where God especially equips an individual and turns up the volume, so to speak.

You may or may not have a notion as to what gifts you have actually been given. Here are some clues to help you: Perhaps you are extra sensitive to the pain and hurt of others—you may have the "gift of mercy." If you often feel compelled to give to others, you just might have the "gift of giving." If you are always the first one to jump up and offer a helping hand, you quite possibly have the "gift of service." If you find that others are frequently drawn to you for godly advice, you probably have the "gift of wisdom." I'm sure you're getting the gist of it.

If you are uncertain at this point, there are actually tests online that can assist you in figuring out your gifting. After answering a series of questions, the survey will narrow down the results to reveal your areas of strength. After discovering your gifts, the time comes for unwrapping, appreciating, and using them. A gift that's never opened or used is, well, useless. Open your gift and let it equip you to fulfill your purpose within the church. A gift is still useless though, unless it's kept wrapped in love.

1 Corinthians 13:13, "And now these three remain: faith, hope and love. But the greatest of these is love."

For more information about spiritual gifts see:

1 Corinthians 12-13

Romans 12

Ephesians 4

Use Me

Finding our purpose within the church can happen quite naturally; it did for me. When my first-born was a toddler I would drop him off each week for his Sunday school class, and each week I was given a tag with a number that corresponded with the one taped to my son's back. In case of emergencies—crying, dirty diapers, and such—they would page parents by flashing your number on the screen at the front of the sanctuary. So, each week I would drop my little guy off, and take my seat in church hoping not to see my number pop up, but week after week it did. It seems my son was experiencing a bit of separation anxiety from me, so each week I would get up from my seat and find my way to his class, where I would stay for the rest of the service. I quickly became a "helper" in the two-year-old room. This was my first foray into ministry. I then began serving alternately in the newborns room to be with my younger son as well. As my boys grew and moved onto Kindergarten, then 1st grade, 2nd grade and so on, I moved along with them. I signed up to volunteer in their classes a couple of times each month. Then I branched out and became a leader at youth group every Wednesday night. I graduated to being a head teacher for the 4/5th Saturday night service. As we reached the middle school years I began to sense that my time with the boys was coming to a close, and I started praying for God to show me my new role within the church. I prayed fervently for Him to grow me, use me, and "enlarge my territory."

1 Chronicles 4:10, "Jabez cried out to the God of Israel, 'Oh, that you would bless me indeed and enlarge my territory! Let your hand be with me, and

keep me from harm so that I will be free from pain.' And God granted his request."

Very soon afterward I was asked to lead a class in our church's women's ministry, where I still serve today. God has continued to grow me exponentially through the privilege of serving His women, and His church. I am doing things I would have never dreamed possible, but with the gifting, equipping, and opportunities I've received from God, I am fulfilling His purpose for me.

You see, I didn't have any special qualifications, other than being willing and ready to answer God's call— He literally called me by flashing my number across the screen.

On my own, I'm just a weak and empty vessel, but with God I am so much more! And so are you. Be on the lookout for any opportunities that God may be flashing across the screen for you. Pray for His guidance, and be faithful and confident as you follow His lead.

Loosely

Whether you're just getting started or have been involved in the church for a long time, remember to hold loosely to your area of ministry—after all, it doesn't really belong to you, it belongs to the Lord. Be open to change in your service to God, following the path that He has for you. Just because you get involved in one area of ministry doesn't mean that is where God will have you plugged in forever. He will move you as He sovereignly sees fit. Serving is not meant to be a burden, and it is not meant to be for your glory, but the Lord's. We are meant to experience *His joy* as we serve alongside Him, in *His ministry*.

Ephesians 2:8-9, "For it is by grace you have been saved, through faith—and this is not from yourselves, it is the gift of God— 9 not by works, so that no one can boast.

Willing

God wants us to stop focusing on our weaknesses and start looking to our strengths—there we will find an outlet for our ultimate purpose of loving others and worshipping Him.

We don't need to search for some grandiose, larger-than-life expression of our purpose, we just have to look at what comes naturally—things we're good at, things we like to do, things that are on our heart, and the things and people we already have access to. It's that simple.

God doesn't use perfect people, He uses willing people. It's not about our ability, but our availability.

2 Corinthians 4:7, "But we have this treasure in jars of clay to show that this all-surpassing power is from God and not from us."

Juggler

Women by nature are the most incredible jugglers. I'm not talking about knives, flaming torches, or balls, but something much more dramatic: they expertly and delicately juggle very complicated lives. Some women juggle crying babies, busy toddlers, and deserving hubbies, and still manage to wash their own hair once a week. Some women are at the other end of the spectrum tending to elderly parents, accompanying them to doctors' appointments while fitting in their own long list of to-do's. Others juggle jobs outside the home during the day, run errands after work, put dinner on the table and a load of wash in the machine all before collapsing into bed at night. Still others dabble in a little of everything by working from home, managing the household, running committees, serving in church, raising kids and then sending them off to college, and all the while keeping the spark in their marriages alive. And so much more. It's no wonder we are worn out! We are not the first of our gender to multitask. Take a look at the Proverbs 31 woman and you'll see she's much the same as you and me, but she doesn't seem at all stressed. I firmly believe it's because she finds strength in the Lord. That's the only way to deal with all that's on our plates while remaining calm and balanced, patient and kind. The Lord must be at the center of it all. The only way we can be "clothed with strength and dignity, and laugh at the days to come," (Proverbs 31:25) without losing ourselves or our minds is to be clothed in the peace of God. I think we'd be wise to come before the Lord each morning, before our juggling act begins, praying for God's strength, joy, peace, and patience, and some wisdom in organizing our day, and in knowing which balls it would ok to drop.

Proverbs 31:25-29, "She is clothed with strength and dignity; she can laugh at the days to come. [26] She speaks with wisdom, and faithful instruction is on her tongue. [27] She watches over the affairs of her household and does not eat the bread of idleness. [28] Her children arise and call her blessed; her husband also, and he praises her: [29] "Many women do noble things, but you surpass them all."

Every Day

Reading about the woman in Proverbs 31 can lead us to a place of discouragement or it can more positively help us to see that valuable purpose is found in our everyday living—our family, our household, our work, our tasks, our words, and our encounters. She was a woman who invested her time wisely and the blessings that followed were evident to everyone. And although she was a married woman with children in tow, these Scriptures speak volumes and offer encouragement of worth to us all.

She is spoken of as a woman of noble character; bringing good to others—not harm; providing food and comfort for her loved ones; being fair and generous; she's described as a hard worker, strong and determined; she is thoughtful and wise; giving to the poor and helping the needy; she's an entrepreneur in her own right, creative in her ventures; she's good with her hands and keeps them joyfully busy. People call her blessed, respecting her integrity, and praising her love for the Lord.

Proverbs 31:30-31, "Charm is deceptive, and beauty is fleeting; but a woman who fears the LORD is to be praised. 31 Honor her for all that her hands have done, and let her works bring her praise at the city gate."

All of these things are highly attainable for ordinary gals like you and me. Our day-to-day living can reflect the same beauty and honor amidst the seemingly mundane. The Lord was her focal point from which everything else flowed, from that she found her strength and for that she was praised. We can do the same. Let's be women of noble character, clothing ourselves in dignity and persevering in God's strength.

Hospitality

Hospitality is an excellent way to live and love like Jesus—He lived a life of invitation everywhere He went, and in doing so the Father was gloriously magnified. We too can see hospitality as our way of serving, and loving as our way of life. Let's welcome others in the name of the Lord—remembering that we are made in the image of Christ.

Whatever I do, whoever I serve, I do it as if for the Lord Himself.

Lord, help me to be humbly open and extravagantly generous with others, just as You are with me. Empower me to be gracious and seize every opportunity to show the love of Jesus. Help me to raise others up and invite them in, just as You do for me. Amen.

Romans 12:13, "Share with the Lord's people who are in need. Practice hospitality."

A Reason

You are saved

Because of His love,

By His power,

For His purpose.

You are saved for a reason.

Exodus 9:16, "But I have raised you up for this very purpose, that I might show you my power and that my name might be proclaimed in all the earth."

2 Timothy 1:9, "He has saved us and called us to a holy life—not because of anything we have done but because of his own purpose and grace. This grace was given us in Christ Jesus before the beginning of time,"

You are Strong

Your strength comes from holding tight to the Lord, so cling to Him with all your might. God promises to never let you down. Be on your guard against the enemy though; he will try to lie to you and say you're all alone. If you let him he will feed your insecurities and play upon your fears: the fear that you're unloved, unwanted, or undesirable; the fear of rejection and abandonment; of not being capable; and most of all he wants you to give in to the fear and believe the lie that you are anything but strong. He knows that if he can weaken your confidence and paralyze you with all these fears you'll no longer be a threat to him. Don't let that wily devil win, don't believe his lies or give in to your fears. Know without a doubt that whatever struggle you're facing, you're not facing it alone. When you find yourself in circumstances beyond your control, when you're being pushed to your limit, or find yourself face-to-face with the unknown, remember that you are the King's daughter. It's your relationship to Him that supplies all the strength you need.

Psalm 63:8, "I cling to You; Your right hand upholds me."

My Confidence

2 Corinthians 3:3-5, "Such confidence we have through Christ before God. ⁵ Not that we are competent in ourselves to claim anything for ourselves, but our competence comes from God."

My confidence is not precariously based on my own ability; it's firmly planted on the Lord and all He does for me. On my own I could never gain salvation, I could never overcome my sin, I could never change my habits, and I most definitely could never face the enemy head-on. But with the Lord by my side I can do all these things and more; with His power at work in me my competence is exponential, my confidence is sure, and my eternal fate secure. Thank you, Lord, for blessing me and empowering me. My confidence is found in only You. Amen.

Security

I looked up the synonyms for the word "security," and here are a few that stood out from among all that I found:

Care, covenant, defense, freedom, guard, pledge, promise, redemption, refuge, retreat, safeguard, safekeeping, salvation, sanctuary, shelter, shield, surety.

The antonyms, as you could guess, stood in sharp contrast:

Harm, hurt, injury, danger, peril, trouble, uncertainty, worry.

All of the synonyms clearly speak of the security we find with the Lord, while the antonyms warn of the trouble we face when we are far from His strong arms. When we know that we are eternally secure we can more bravely face any potential harms that will likely cross our paths. We're more willing to take a leap of faith because we're assured we have a safe place to land. We're more willing to step out of our comfort zone, because the Lord is our shield wherever we go. Knowing all the security we have gives us strength to stand and faith to fly.

Your Heavenly Father holds you secure in the palm of His hand...and "no one can snatch you out."

John 10:28, "I give them eternal life, and they shall never perish; no one will snatch them out of my hand."

(Synonyms and antonyms were found on www.Thesaurus.com.)

Quieted

Zephaniah 3:17, "The LORD your God in your midst,
The Mighty One, will save;
He will rejoice over you with gladness,
He will quiet you with His love,
He will rejoice over you with singing." NKJV

Reading this lovely verse takes me back to my childhood: I remember being at the dining room table, sitting on my Grandma's lap, cradled in my Grandma's strong arms; I remember the sound of her tender voice as she rocked me back and forth singing me to sleep, and how the chair she sat upon seemed to squeak in rhythm with her precious lullabies. In the warmth of her love and the safety of her presence my mind quieted, and my body found rest. So similar, but on a much grander scale is the comfort we find in the Presence of God. While the world around us swirls and shakes, God is inviting us to climb onto His lap, rest in His mighty arms, and be quieted by the sound of His voice and His gentle love.

Simply Wait

When an issue arises our first response is usually to lace up our shoes and start running to and fro, frantically trying to fix and figure everything out on our own. God stops us in our tracks and tells us to simply wait upon Him and witness what only He can do. It takes great faith and a whole lot of restraint to give control to the Lord, even though we know He is good. Don't rush ahead, take a breath and take heart, look to the Lord and find strength. In His perfect timing and in His sovereign way everything will ultimately be worked out.

Psalm 27:13-14, "I remain confident of this: I will see the goodness of the LORD in the land of the living. ¹⁴ Wait for the LORD; be strong and take heart and wait for the LORD."

In Gratitude

Of all the places you search for strength, gratitude should be high on the list. If you feel like you're losing your can-do spirit, take a moment to reflect and see if you've been counting your blessings enough. Nothing will bring encouragement and renewed strength like reflecting on all of your blessings and on God's faithfulness and power in your life. When you feel down, look up; when you feel weak, remember God's strength; when you're discouraged, be encouraged by the promises of God. When you're done counting your blessings, recount them again. Let gratitude fortify your heart, soul, and mind.

Colossians 3:16, "Let the message of Christ dwell among you richly as you teach and admonish one another with all wisdom through psalms, hymns, and songs from the Spirit, singing to God with gratitude in your hearts."

Contented

Being discontent steals our joy, misdirects our focus, and causes us to grumbles and complain, infecting everyone around. Being content is like a soothing balm upon the soul; it is anchored on the knowledge that the Lord is in control. Being content brings a joy that can't be stolen. Throughout our lifetimes we'll encounter both good times and bad; being content keeps our feet on solid ground and helps us endure all the ups and downs. Content in the arms of our Lord and in the center of His will is where I always want to be.

Philippians 4:12-13, "I know what it is to be in need, and I know what it is to have plenty. I have learned the secret of being content in any and every situation, whether well fed or hungry, whether living in plenty or in want. ¹³ I can do all this through him who gives me strength."

Powerful

When you feel powerless, I encourage you to read and reread the verses below. You my dear, are anything but powerless—you are extraordinarily powerful.

You have been filled up and given access to the power of Christ. Don't neglect to tap into it and let it guide, empower, and change your life.

Scripture claims that the same mighty power God exerted and miraculously displayed by raising Jesus to life from the grips of the grave, and then seating Him in Heaven to sovereignly rule for all of eternity, is also at work *for us* who believe. Take a moment to reflect with awe and wonder on the enormous grandeur of what God accomplished through the life, death, and resurrection of our Savior.

That same power works *for us*: saving us from eternal death, sin, and condemnation. His power brings us forgiveness, eternal life, and freedom.

That same power works *in us*: renewing, transforming, invigorating, refreshing, and strengthening us. His power gives us a new perspective, fresh hope, a bold confidence. His power changes us from the inside out.

That same power works *through us*: equipping us to impact our family, friends, and the world around us with His message of salvation and His remarkably extravagant love.

Ephesians 1:18-23, "I pray that the eyes of your heart may be enlightened in order that you may know the hope to which he has called you, the riches of his glorious inheritance in his holy people, [19] and his incomparably great power for us who believe. That power is the same as the mighty strength [20] he exerted when he raised Christ from the dead and seated him at his right hand in the heavenly realms, [21] far above all rule and authority, power and dominion, and every name that is invoked, not only in the present age but also in the one to come. [22] And God placed all things under his feet and appointed him to be head over everything for the church, [23] which is his body, the fullness of him who fills everything in every way."

Sufficient

There are so many obstacles we try to face and seek to change all on our own, many of these are things that simply can't be overcome alone. But with the strength of Jesus and the power of the Holy Spirit working in us we can.

Through His mighty power we are able to:

- Overcome sin
- Forgive others
- Forgive ourselves
- Stand strong in our convictions
- Face persecution
- Persevere triumphantly
- Endure pain and suffering
- Have hope even in grief
- Resist temptation
- Love difficult people
- Hold our tongue
- Conquer fear
- Calm anxiety
- Step out of depression
- Change our negative thinking
- Break free from addiction
- Transform a bad attitude
- Let go of bitterness
- Experience healing
- Obey the LORD
- Stand victorious
- Etc.

Everything that has been invited in or has slyly crept into our lives over the years, every unwanted guest that has made itself at home in our hearts and minds, can be confidently kicked to the curb. Our new lives in Christ have no room for these anymore.

God's power provides all we need for righteous and victorious living. Keep connected to His power through constant prayer, daily Bible reading, regular meditation on His Word and promises—claim them for yourself.

Invite God to powerfully move in your life and strengthen you to overcome anything that stood out on the previous list or any other obstacles that come to your mind. Draw on His power that is at work in you!

2 Peter 1:3, "His divine power has given us everything we need for a godly life through our knowledge of him who called us by his own glory and goodness."

Winning Side

There is a war raging all around us. It is an unseen, spiritual war. Satan is the instigator, initiator, and evil, rebellious force behind this battle. In his awful pride he has pitted himself against God Almighty, Jesus Christ, and all of Jesus' followers. Satan's whole purpose is to keep people from accepting Jesus Christ as their Savior and receiving eternal life. If you have accepted Christ then you have already won the war, and are safe and secure in the hands of God for all of eternity. Although we are on the winning side, we will still endure attacks. We have a choice as to the part we will play in the ongoing battles: the helpless victim, or the powerful warrior that we truly are in Christ. Attacks will come in various ways—physical, spiritual, emotional, mental. Satan knows our eternal fate is secure but he wants to disrupt and destroy our daily life by making us feel defeated, and anything but strong. He desperately wants to steer our focus off of God and steal the gloriously victorious life that is rightfully ours in Christ.

God always wins and the war with Satan is no exception. We are on the winning side. Let that Biblical truth sink in and fill you with confidence as you head into combat.

Deuteronomy 28:7, "The LORD will grant that the enemies who rise up against you will be defeated before you. They will come at you from one direction but flee from you in seven."

Authority

When I was a young girl my grandparents would often take my two cousins and me to their cabin in the mountains for weekend retreats. Around their cabin were acres of woods in which we would walk and explore. On one such hike I distinctly remember a lesson my Grandma taught me using bears for her illustration. She quite simply told me that if a bear were to emerge out of the trees and come towards us we should stop and immediately begin to pray, calling aloud on the Name of Jesus, and binding Satan and any attacks he would bring our way. I have tucked this little story into my heart and keep it ready on my mind. *Bears*, you see, can come in various forms; they're not just the furry guys roaming the woods. *Bears* can represent any of the conflicts, confrontations, and dangers we may encounter. I find my Grandma's lesson very practical for any physical, emotional, and spiritual attacks I may face. Her lesson taught me this amazing truth: as a child of God I am in the privileged position to call on the name and power of Jesus to defend me, and I am also in the position to stand in confident authority against Satan and his schemes.

2 Timothy 1:7, "For God has not given us a spirit of fear, but of power and of love and of a sound mind." NKJV

Undefeated

Sitting on my bathroom counter is a picture of a woman who though I have never met, inspires me beyond measure. I look at her every morning as I get ready to greet the day and as I retire to the comfort of my bed at the evening's end. Behind this snapshot, there is the story so surreal, that I wouldn't have believed it if I hadn't seen it for myself. To the observer this picture is merely a woman standing in front of the Duomo in Florence, Italy. It is one of the largest cathedrals in the world, and the small figure in my photograph stands dwarfed in its shadow. As we walked through the piazza on the day represented, the sound of goose-bump-inducing opera filled the air. Before we even saw her, the melody of her divine voice caught our ears. As we rounded the corner the sight of her precious unassuming frame caught our eyes. Seated on the ground before her was a crowd of listeners enjoying the impromptu performance. It was truly a treat for the senses. As I stood watching and listening, I became aware of the grace and power, humility and quiet courage, all blended together, that seemingly flowed from deep within her. As her voice rang out, tears welled in my eyes. The beauty was overwhelming and unexpected. And just as unexpected was the abrupt, ugly, mocking interruption that came from a balcony, three stories above. Much to my astonishment, and more to my dismay, a real-life operatic enactment of the age old, epic battle between good and evil began to play out before my very eyes. This older man with a super snug, white undershirt stretched across his bulging belly, leaned out of his window, opened his loud mouth, and erupted into the most horribly mean-spirited singing I've ever heard. He spewed out his own jeering rendition in response to her sonnet. The more she pressed on, the louder he got. He was undeniably under the influence of way-too-many alcoholic beverages.

124

Despite this madman's attempts to discourage and defeat her, my precious woman-in-the-picture pressed on—much to the crowd's pleasure and applause. She was determined—a woman of persevering strength, focused on her passion and her purpose. There was no hesitation, not even for a moment. He could not dissuade or stop her, no matter how hard he tried, and boy did he try. She pressed on holding her head high, doing what she had set out to do that day.

This real-life earthly event perfectly portrayed the spiritual battle taking place in the heavenly realm, and all around us, every day. So often the enemy takes aim directly at us. The moment we're doing what we're gifted for and called to do, evil steps in to discourage us. The mocking voice seeks to cause doubt, spewing, "You're not good enough," and, "Why even try?" It says, "Just give up, nobody cares anyway." Lies, lies, lies—meant to keep us from all the blessings God has in store, and all that He wants to use us for. The enemy's tactics are outright ugly, like the man behind the scenes of my picture. But we shine brightly when we press on, determined to trust in God. Persevere, stand undefeated; don't let evil win. God's approval is what matters most; It's His applause we seek, but sometimes in the process others will take notice and cheer us on with pleasure too.

Ephesians 6:10-12, "Finally, be strong in the Lord and in his mighty power. [11] Put on the full armor of God, so that you can take your stand against the devil's schemes. [12] For our struggle is not against flesh and blood, but against the rulers, against the authorities, against the powers of this dark world and against the spiritual forces of evil in the heavenly realms."

God's Armor

Ephesians 6:13-17, "Therefore put on the full armor of God, so that when the day of evil comes, you may be able to stand your ground, and after you have done everything, to stand. Stand firm then, with the belt of truth buckled around your waist, with the breastplate of righteousness in place, [15] and with your feet fitted with the readiness that comes from the gospel of peace. [16] In addition to all this, take up the shield of faith, with which you can extinguish all the flaming arrows of the evil one. [17] Take the helmet of salvation and the sword of the Spirit, which is the word of God."

God Himself provides the armor we need for battle and in standing against the enemy's schemes, but it's up to us to consciously put it on. These verses are filled with commands for action—put on, stand firm, take up. The power of God's armor is readily available to us, yet we have an active part in its effectiveness. If it's not utilized, it's useless. These Scriptures encourage us to get ready and stay ready for the battles up ahead. Put on the armor each and every day; readjust, tighten, and secure any areas that come loosened. Each piece of the armor has a unique function, yet overlaps and interweaves with the others forming an impenetrable barrier. Dressed in God's armor we become mighty warriors, protected and empowered by the Lord.

The Belt of Truth

Truth marks God's children as set apart for Him, and different from the world. Putting on the Belt of Truth means basing and building our lives on what God says about literally anything and everything. God's Truth is the *only* truth that is unchanging, unwavering, solid, and eternal. His Truth brings much needed stability to our lives, being that it isn't based on our ever-changing emotions, feelings, desires, perspective, or on society's fickle standard. God's Truth is objective, holy, pure, good, and perfect. Putting on the Belt of Truth means anchoring our life to God's perspective and standard, and judging all else accordingly. The enemy would love to get us off track from Truth—he's always ready to feed us a lie. If you are ever uncertain of what Truth really is, just open your Bible for a solid reminder. The Belt of Truth is the first piece of armor we put on, and it's the Truth to which all the other pieces are anchored.

John 14:6, "Jesus answered, 'I am the way and the truth and the life. No one comes to the Father except through me.'"

The Breastplate of Righteousness

Righteousness is the practical application of Truth in our lives. It is the act of living out our new identity in Christ with purity according to God's perfect Word. In a nutshell, the Breastplate of Righteousness is put on every time we choose to align our lives to God's holy ways. Unchecked sin is like holes in our armor. Our sins become places left unsecured, open, vulnerable, and the enemy sees these as a welcome invitation to launch his attack. Right living seals our armor up tight, rendering it impenetrable, removing opportunities for regret, shame, or condemnation. God knows what He is saying, when He tells us to live right. As our loving Father He truly wants to protect us from harm.

Leviticus 19:2, "Therefore, be holy, as I am holy."

Shoes of the Gospel of Peace

Through the death, burial, and resurrection of Jesus Christ we have peace with God—that is the Gospel (the Good News) made short and so sweet. Through Jesus the obstacles of sin, death, and condemnation are removed from us forever. We have a direct line of communication with our Heavenly Father. Jesus has removed the enmity and hostility which previously kept us from Him, giving us *peace with God*. Through Jesus Christ we also have been bestowed with the additional blessing of the *peace of God*. You may be asking what the difference is in this minute variation of wording. Well, simply put, the *peace of God* is the peace that surpasses all human understanding and doesn't make any sense. It is a settled assurance within our soul that everything is going to be OK, despite our current circumstances. Satan loves nothing more than to get us all worked up and bring turmoil into our hearts and minds, but with the *peace of God* we are equipped to remain steady and unshaken by the events and issues that are attacking us. Our peace *with* God and *of* God equips us to go out and *share His message of peace with a chaotic world.*

Philippians 4:7, "And the peace of God, which transcends all understanding, will guard your hearts and your minds in Christ Jesus."

129

Shield of Faith

Faith is *believing and acting* on God's Truth (hence the saying, "step out in faith.") It is trusting in God's ability and taking Him at His Word. Faith is believing what God says over what we can see—it is seeing the possible, in the impossible. A mindset of faith leaves no room for worry or fear. A mindset of faith has to be purposefully and continually chosen. Faith is claiming that if God says it, then it must be true. Lack of faith is the biggest hindrance to the abundant life God has for each of us—that's why Satan constantly whispers notions of doubt. The shield of faith extinguishes all the flaming arrows of doubt that the enemy shoots at us.

Psalm 84:11-12, "For the LORD God is a sun and shield, the LORD bestows favor and honor; no good thing does he withhold from those whose walk is blameless. ¹² LORD Almighty, blessed is the one who trusts in you."

Helmet of Salvation

Salvation represents who we are in Christ—saved and redeemed, fresh and new, set free, a child of God. The helmet of Salvation protects our mind from the lies regarding our identity that try to infiltrate and destroy. Satan greatly desires that we forget who we really are, and all the benefits that have been given to us. If we forget we are *a daughter of the King*, and that we have access to the heavenly resources of God, then Satan is definitely at an advantage over us. Salvation is not only what we are saved *from* (the wrath and judgment of God), but also what we are saved *to*—free and abundant life here on earth, glorious eternal life in Heaven.

Galatians 5:1, "It is for freedom that Christ has set us free. Stand firm, then, and do not let yourselves be burdened again by a yoke of slavery."

Sword of the Spirit (the Word of God)

The Sword of the Spirit is both a defensive and offensive weapon that is ours to confidently wield, in fighting back any attacks and lies from the enemy. Any time he speaks untruths to us we are to immediately *turn our thoughts to the encouragements that God has spoken personally to us through His Word*—the words that have popped off the page at us, the words that were spoken in a church service that we know were meant just for us, the words that we've tucked securely into our hearts. The Word of God has power in our lives—the power to save us, change us, comfort us, encourage us, teach us, admonish us, lead us, and the power to refute the lies of the enemy. God's Word is living and active.

Hebrews 4:12, "For the word of God is alive and active. Sharper than any double-edged sword, it penetrates even to dividing soul and spirit, joints and marrow; it judges the thoughts and attitudes of the heart."

Identity

2 Corinthians 10:4-5, "The weapons we fight with are not the weapons of the world. On the contrary, they have divine power to demolish strongholds. 5 We demolish arguments and every pretension that sets itself up against the knowledge of God, and we take captive every thought to make it obedient to Christ."

The Armor of God is simply your identity in Christ. Stand firm in who God is and in who you are—you are loved, you are forgiven and new, you belong, you matter, you are beautiful, you have purpose, you are strong, and you are royalty. You are a daughter of the King, you are a child of God. Use that truth to tear down the lies.

Ephesians 6:10, "Finally, be strong in the Lord and in his mighty power."

Pray

Ephesians 6:18, "And pray in the Spirit on all occasions with all kinds of prayers and requests. With this in mind, be alert and always keep on praying for all the Lord's people."

Prayer is our direct line of communication with The God of the Universe. Prayer invites the Lord, exalted high on the throne, into our situation, and asks Him to powerfully move. He moves for us, in us, and through us. When we pray we acknowledge His authority and encounter His power. When we pray it opens the door between God's heart and ours; it bridges the gap between His strength and ours.

Let's pray for boldness and courage and strength. Let's pray for hope and joy and peace, to take fear's place. Let's pray for the faith to step out of the chains and walk out the prison doors He's already unlocked. Let's pray extraordinary prayers, then stand back and watch God accomplish what's possible only through Him. Let's pray all the time with heartfelt requests, always asking God to align them with His will. Let's be alert to what's going on around us, all the while keeping our eyes focused and our voices lifted to Jesus. This, my dear sister, is the greatest piece of armor.

Faithful One

My confidence is built on nothing less than God's goodness and faithfulness. My faith is rooted in the One who is steadfastly faithful, even when I am not. My faith often falters when tested beyond what I can see right in front me, yet His faithfulness extends beyond the skies above, going on forever and ever. That is why my strength is found in Him. I know that He will never let me down.

Psalm 36:5, "Your love, LORD, reaches to the heavens, your faithfulness to the skies."

Conquerors

The love of God makes us conquerors in more ways than we can ever count—His love saves, His love lives, His love guides and admonishes, His love refreshes and comforts, His love protects, His love strengthens. Whenever we feel weak or powerless we need only reflect on the sacrificial love that the Father has lavished on us.

Romans 8:37, "We are more than conquerors through Him who loved us."

Hope

Isaiah 40:31, "but those who hope in the LORD will renew their strength. They will soar on wings like eagles; they will run and not grow weary, they will walk and not be faint."

The key to not being defeated is keeping your mind and heart set on *hope*. You have been given promises of great hope—you are saved, you are redeemed, you have the Holy Spirit to guide and comfort you, you have the hope of Heaven for all of eternity, you have Jesus with you each and every moment, you have hope in knowing that your trials on earth are but a tiny blip in the timeline of eternity. Hope, my dear friend, is recognizing Jesus in the moment and clinging to Him for strength in your hour of need, while still holding onto hope that with Jesus there is always something better on the horizon.

Hope restores life.

Hope is the tender voice of God calling us onward.

Breathes

My battles are not won on my own. They are won when the Holy Spirit of God begins to move—the same Spirit that commands the waves to surge, the winds to blow, the mountains to quake, the sun to rise, the stars to shine is at work in me and for me. Through this exact Spirit I gain my strength; I find refreshment as He breathes new life to my weary bones. He steadies my feet and fortifies my soul; it is through His power alone that I can do it all.

Zechariah 4:6, "'Not by might nor by power, but by my Spirit,' says the LORD Almighty."

Anointed

Psalm 23:1-6, "The LORD is my shepherd, I lack nothing. ² He makes me lie down in green pastures, he leads me beside quiet waters,³ he refreshes my soul. He guides me along the right paths for his name's sake. ⁴ Even though I walk through the darkest valley, I will fear no evil, for you are with me; your rod and your staff, they comfort me.⁵ You prepare a table before me in the presence of my enemies. You anoint my head with oil; my cup overflows. ⁶ Surely your goodness and love will follow me all the days of my life, and I will dwell in the house of the LORD forever."

Lord, You are so good to me. Despite trials and tribulations that inevitably come up, I know that peace can always be found with You. You give me perfect rest and restore my weary soul. You place me in a meadow so I can run barefoot in the grass. You lead me to a bubbling brook so I can dip my hands in the cool water and scoop it up for a sip. You are my flashlight in the darkest of night; You hold my hand and won't let go. You throw me a banquet and feed me a feast, even while trouble circles on all sides. You anoint my head with oil, washing away the blackened ashes of fear, replacing them with calm, wiping away my every tear. In Your Presence I find an abundance of blessings, which my heart can hardly contain. I know that You are always with me, and Your love follows wherever I go, every single day. Amen.

You are Royalty

Even in my adult years I am fascinated by the royalty of far off lands. There is something fantastically magical in the idea of a royal family. I'm pretty sure I'm not the only one who feels this way. Princess gowns complete with tiaras are often a little girl's delight. Millions tune in to watch the televised fairytale weddings of the British monarchy, oohing and ahhing over the prince and his princess bride. But there is no need or room for envy:

If God is the King of Glory and Jesus is the King of Kings, and we are daughters of the King, that means we are royalty in the highest sense; we are princesses in the Kingdom of God. We have at our disposal and are invited to enjoy all the benefits, privileges, and honor as daughters of the King. Our Father is not just any king, but King over all of heaven and earth—it doesn't get any more royal than that!

Psalm 24:10, "Who is He, this King of glory? The LORD Almighty—He is the King of glory."

Perfect

Since God is absolutely perfect you can be assured His Kingdom is perfect too. It is very unlike any kingdom on earth—any that has ever been or ever will be. It is otherworldly, so different from what we know and experience in our day-to-day lives. The Kingdom of God isn't tangled up in the momentary things of earth; it is focused on the eternal things of God—things that will last forever and ever. God's Kingdom is described as an everlasting, heavenly Kingdom, in authority over every other kingdom of this world; it is a place of safety, ruled with God's perfect justice, filled with an atmosphere of righteousness, peace and joy. Scripture calls it a kingdom that can't ever be shaken, and will remain firm forever—having experienced California earthquakes, I love that idea. As *daughters of the King*, you and I are graciously invited and welcomed to take our place in this perfect Kingdom of God.

2 Peter 1:11, "and you will receive a rich welcome into the eternal kingdom of our Lord and Savior Jesus Christ."

Humility

Our entrance into the Kingdom of God isn't dependent upon our performance; it's not based on our power, influence, or popularity; it's not based on our wealth, the size of our hips, or our bank account. We are granted entrance only by the grace of God. Completely opposite to what the world requires of us, He sees our weaknesses and says, "I want you." The Kingdom of God flips many of mankind's philosophies upside-down, turning them on their head. God sees our weaknesses as positive strengths, as great opportunities for Him to go to work. Pride and arrogance have no place in God's Kingdom; when entering His Holy Presence, humility is where it's at.

James 4:10, "Humble yourselves before the Lord, and he will lift you up."

Poor

Matthew 5: 1-3, "Now when Jesus saw the crowds, he went up on a mountainside and sat down. His disciples came to him, ² and he began to teach them.

He said: ³ 'Blessed are the poor in spirit, for theirs is the kingdom of heaven.'"

Being *poor in spirit* is the only thing required for our entrance into the Kingdom of Heaven. It is our first step into a relationship with God. Recognizing that on our own we are destitute and can never earn our way or measure up to God's perfect standard isn't a bad thing, but actually extremely good. It puts our hearts in a place where we are willing to fully surrender and completely rely on God. Being *poor in spirit* is coming face-to-face with our inadequacies, our spiritual deficits, and acknowledging our desperate need for a Savior. Being *poor in spirit* is the essential key to unlocking abundant blessings, causing the doors of Heaven to swing open wide.

Mourner

Matthew 5:4, "'Blessed are those who mourn, for they will be comforted.'"

When we surrender our lives to Christ our sins suddenly stand out in sharp contrast to His perfect holiness, causing us to *mourn* what we see in ourselves. Having placed our faith in Jesus for our salvation and our way into the Kingdom, we become all-too-aware of our sinful nature. The ugliness of our sin brings sorrow, which leads us to repentance, which then leads us to the grace, mercy, and forgiveness of our loving Father. In this way, *mourning* brings great comfort and gladness!

Meek

Matthew 5:5, "'Blessed are the meek, for they will inherit the earth.'"

Don't confuse *meekness* with weakness. Usually when we hear the word meekness we imagine a quiet mouse or a doormat that's walked all over, but this is so not the case—it means anything but that. When Jesus walked this earth He perfectly exemplified *meekness*. He was and is extremely powerful and mighty, yet Scripture also uses words such as gentle and humble to describe Him. He exhibited this balanced blend of attributes by giving His will over to the Father's control. He could have done anything He wanted but surrendered Himself to God's Sovereign plan, even to the extent of sacrificing His life for us. So, with Jesus as our example, what does *meekness* look like in own lives? It simply means that we also humbly surrender ourselves to the Father's plan by seeking Him and His ways for the course of our own lives. We can confidently surrender because we know who God is, and who we are in Him. Being a *meek* child of God means being confident in our identity, but knowing it all comes from God. Through *meekness*, the Scriptures tell us, we not only inherit the Kingdom of God, we also inherit the earth.

Hungry

Matthew 5:6, "'Blessed are those who hunger and thirst for righteousness, for they will be filled.'"

Jesus is the only *righteous* One—the only One truly perfect in God's eyes—to ever walk this earth. Don't get discouraged, but Scripture says our righteousness is like dirty rags before the LORD (Isaiah 64:6). Even on our best day, we could never clean ourselves up enough to be deemed right in God's eyes. Now here's some encouragement: fortunately, because of Jesus' sacrifice and our faith in Him, God sees us through the covering of Jesus' righteousness. Since God sees us this way, we're now inspired to pursue the righteous standing that we've already been given. To *hunger*, is to yearn to become more and more like our Savior. To *thirst*, is to crave for His *righteousness* to take over and reign in us. When the cry of our heart and our soul's pining is for more of God, He will undoubtedly answer our prayers and satisfy our vacancy inside.

Merciful

Matthew 5:7, "'Blessed are the merciful, for they will be shown mercy.'"

We have come to what may be the most difficult of the *Beatitudes* to which we must surrender. The verses on the preceding pages relate to the relationship between us and God, while this one focuses on the relationship between us and others. Being *merciful* may be hard sometimes, but as we follow through out of obedience, the blessings from God will surely follow. A huge benefit of forgiveness is that a heart full of mercy is freed from the gnawing of bitterness.

Recognizing the undeserved mercy that God has bestowed on us should make it much easier to show mercy to other undeserving folks who are much like ourselves. As we extend mercy to others we are expressing our understanding, appreciation, and gratitude for the mercy God has generously given us. If you are a recipient of God's mercy, ask Him to help you release your grudges, freeing you up to extend that same mercy to others.

Pure

Matthew 5:8, "'Blessed are the pure in heart, for they will see God.'"

To see God means to perceive, discern, be aware of Him, and to experience His Presence fully. In order to see God our hearts must be pure. To truly see Him, our hearts have to be free of contaminants and debris. A heart is made pure and is spotlessly cleansed the moment we meet Jesus, but keeping it clean and free of impurities is a continual process. The best way to keep our hearts pure is to run everything through the filter of our relationship with God. Filter everything that comes in, because it affects everything that goes out. Much of what we allow in can harden our hearts, clog our ears, and obscure our vision of God; things such as bitterness, hatred, anger, fear, worry, anxiety, pride, etc., can distort God's voice and make us feel distant from Him. However, when we allow His love to filter and cleanse such rubbish, we're able to gaze unhindered at His glory as the invisible Presence of God suddenly becomes quite clear.

Peacemaker

Matthew 5:9, "'Blessed are the peacemakers, for they will be called children of God.'"

Our Heavenly Father is the ultimate Peacemaker. He sent His Son, Jesus, to restore peace between Himself and us. We are God's children, and thus carry a strong family resemblance. In the footsteps of our Father, we are entrusted to carry on the family legacy of being peacemakers as well. As children of God we are meant to build bridges to walk across, not walls to keep people out. Bringing peace to this world as representatives of Jesus means we have to let go of our selfish demands and the need for getting our own way, and instead begin following Jesus' commands and seeking His supreme way. Let's reflect on some ways we can introduce others to Jesus so they too can enjoy peace and reconciliation with God. We can begin by opening our hearts and our arms...and then add our words.

Persecuted

Matthew 5:10-12, "'Blessed are those who are persecuted because of righteousness, for theirs is the kingdom of heaven. Blessed are you when people insult you, persecute you and falsely say all kinds of evil against you because of me. [12] Rejoice and be glad, because great is your reward in heaven, for in the same way they persecuted the prophets who were before you.'"

These verses stand in direct opposition to our natural feelings. Normally our first instinct would be to run the other way, or fight back with nastiness when faced with persecution and insults, but Jesus has different advice. Jesus gave us words of encouragement and warned us that just as He faced adversaries, as His followers we will too. Not everyone we encounter will share our affection for Jesus, and they will let us know it. But we don't have to be afraid or let them deflate our confidence, because we have an amazing, victorious award awaiting us in Heaven. For every sharp word spoken or fist launched against us for our devotion to Jesus, there is a counter blessing beyond imagination for us in store. All the persecution and insults we could possibly face here will fade from memory when we stand in the glory of Heaven. It will all be eclipsed by the love and healing of God. So, persevere during your time here on earth, as you cling tightly to the promise of Heaven.

Complete Sense

Right now, we're in a waiting game—our Savior has already come and given His life, making us right with The Father, but that's not the end of the story. Jesus lived and died, was buried in a tomb, but after three days rose to life again conquering sin and the grave forever. After walking amongst His disciples for a time in His resurrected state, He ascended up to Heaven and took His rightful seat on the Throne. Before ascending His last words to His followers held the promise that He will surely return, and at that precise future moment we'll all be transformed. Through His actions we've been set free from our sins and our guilt, gaining forgiveness and eternal life as well. We've been given The Holy Spirit to guide us along, to comfort us, and refine us into the likeness of Christ. For now, it's a daily struggle between our fleshly desires and The Spirit within. Some day though, this struggle will finally end—when Jesus returns for us and we see Him face-to-face everything will finally and completely make sense. We will see Him clearly with all obstacles removed; the battle between our flesh and The Spirit will be over, with The Spirit of God reigning victorious in us forevermore!

1 John 3:2-3, "Dear friends, now we are children of God, and what we will be has not yet been made known. But we know that when Christ appears, we shall be like him, for we shall see him as he is. ³ All who have this hope in him purify themselves, just as he is pure."

Lamp

Every evening the skies put on a miraculous light display—as the sun drops down at the close of day, the moon is on the horizon waiting to take its place, and the stars turn on as if someone has flipped a switch. The beauty of these heavenly bodies catches my eyes and holds my gaze with its glimmer and sparkle, although they are merely a shadow of the blazing Glory of God. When Jesus returns and the earth is renewed, there will no longer be a need for the sun, moon, or stars to shine. The warm radiance of Jesus and God the Father will fill the air with supernatural brightness and beauty, absolutely taking our breath away. The light of God and the lamp of Jesus will guide us both day and night. In their Presence all darkness will be removed; only the Light will remain.

Revelation 21:22-24, "I did not see a temple in the city, because the Lord God Almighty and the Lamb are its temple. 23 The city does not need the sun or the moon to shine on it, for the glory of God gives it light, and the Lamb is its lamp. 24 The nations will walk by its light, and the kings of the earth will bring their splendor into it."

Home Sweet Home

Home. What a beautiful word! It represents a place where we belong and matter; a place where love and warmth abound. For some of us, memories of a childhood home come to mind, for others it's a grandparent's house. For others still, refuge, safety, and comfort were found in the home of a neighbor or friend. Wherever it is that you've felt most welcome and your heart has felt at home, find hope in knowing that Jesus Himself is preparing a heavenly residence to surpass all dwellings you've previously known. At the perfect time He will return and take you to be with Him in your new perfect home.

John 14:1-4, "'Do not let your hearts be troubled. You believe in God; believe also in me. ² My Father's house has many rooms; if that were not so, would I have told you that I am going there to prepare a place for you?³ And if I go and prepare a place for you, I will come back and take you to be with me that you also may be where I am. ⁴ You know the way to the place where I am going.'"

Home is really about the people we find there—and when we get to be with Jesus in Heaven, that'll be the epitome of Home.

Heaven on Earth

Your earthly home may not be perfect; all of us who've spent any time on this earth have undoubtedly encountered pain, suffering, sin, tears, and mourning. But take heart and know that this will all pass away when Jesus brings His Heavenly Kingdom to earth. This world was never meant to completely satisfy. When God created us, He set Heaven upon our hearts. All our yearning will only be satisfied when we see Jesus plainly.

According to Scripture, at the appointed time—which only our Heavenly Father knows—Jesus will return to earth to gather His loved ones to be with Him forever. And at that time, He will also renew the earth, not just back to its original grand state from during the time that Adam and Eve walked in the Garden of Eden, but a gloriously perfect beauty which surpasses anything we've previously seen or can comprehend with our finite minds. Our Lord and Savior will be at the focus and center of it all!

We have hope in our future, and Jesus calls us to persevere with that promised hope in mind—His hope does not disappoint. There is a great reward for those who love Him and are awaiting His return. He is going to make all things new; the earth will no longer be tainted by sin and suffering. The earth will be remade into a dazzling, glorious sight. Safety will be found within the walls of God's Kingdom. We'll never have to lock our doors again, because there will be no violence or fear. Love, peace, and joy will fill the air. Irritations and frustrations of this life will fade in light of what really matters—being with Jesus. Take heart; this heavenly hope is in your future and mine.

There is no need for us to ever fear abandonment with our Lord. If He has promised to return for us, then He most certainly will.

1 Thessalonians 4:16-18, "For the Lord himself will come down from heaven, with a loud command, with the voice of the archangel and with the trumpet call of God, and the dead in Christ will rise first. [17] After that, we who are still alive and are left will be caught up together with them in the clouds to meet the Lord in the air. And so, we will be with the Lord forever. [18] Therefore encourage one another with these words."

Reign

When Jesus returns and sets up His Kingdom, we will finally and completely enjoy the privileges that He came to give us. At that time the realization of our blessed position will come to full fruition. Believers from across the planet and spanning the ages will be gathered together to reign on the earth with Jesus. We will no longer be subjected to harassment from the enemy, or the harshness of the elements; we will be priests to the Living God, and just like in the Garden of Eden (as we were always intended), we will rule in humble authority over the earth. As the redeemed beloved of Christ, we will reign with moral dignity, experience perfect freedom, and bathe in the riches of our inheritance. As followers of Christ we will be given liberty and honor in the glorious Kingdom of God. This never ceases to amaze or humble me.

Revelation 5:9-11, "And they sang a new song, saying:

'You are worthy to take the scroll and to open its seals, because you were slain, and with your blood you purchased for God persons from every tribe and language and people and nation. ¹⁰ You have made them to be a kingdom and priests to serve our God, and they will reign on the earth.'"

Crowned

God would not leave His princess without a beautiful crown to grace her head. In fact, He has crowned you with imperishable blessings which will last forevermore. Unlike man-made crowns, the crown that our Heavenly Father gives will last for all of eternity. It won't ever bend or break, it won't get tarnished or lose a jewel, it can't be lost or stolen. His crown for you is eternal. He crowns your head with honor and glory, love and compassion, everlasting joy, salvation and righteousness; He crowns you with eternal life in return for your faithfulness. We have done nothing of any measure to earn such a priceless treasure; it's given to us only by God's grace. So, the crown we receive will be humbly and gratefully laid at our Savior's beautiful feet, rightfully giving Him all the honor and glory.

Revelation 4:9-11, "Whenever the living creatures give glory, honor and thanks to him who sits on the throne and who lives for ever and ever, 10 the twenty-four elders fall down before him who sits on the throne and worship him who lives for ever and ever. They lay their crowns before the throne and say:

11 'You are worthy, our Lord and God, to receive glory and honor and power, for you created all things, and by your will they were created and have their being.'"

Transformed

Whatever ailments you are presently struggling against, know that they will not last forever. There is hope in the fact that the body you currently have will be gloriously transformed when Jesus returns. The body you live in now is meant for a temporary existence, topping off at around 100 years max. A heavenly, eternal Kingdom calls for a heavenly body that will last for all of eternity. I think of loved ones who've had great pain, handicaps, and diseases during their life on earth, and I have joy in knowing that God will bless them with new—not just restored, but completely new—bodies, that move with ease and freedom. I myself am looking forward to a day of no aching back, no pesky allergies, no reading glasses, and no orthotic inserts in my shoes. I also long for the day when my mind is renewed, and sin and temptation are no longer a struggle. There is perfect renewal in your future, and mine. Can I get an "Amen!" to that?

1 Corinthians 15:50-54, "I declare to you, brothers and sisters, that flesh and blood cannot inherit the kingdom of God, nor does the perishable inherit the imperishable. 51 Listen, I tell you a mystery: We will not all sleep, but we will all be changed— 52 in a flash, in the twinkling of an eye, at the last trumpet. For the trumpet will sound, the dead will be raised imperishable, and we will be changed. 53 For the perishable must clothe itself with the imperishable, and the mortal with immortality. 54 When the perishable has been clothed with

the imperishable, and the mortal with immortality, then the saying that is written will come true: "Death has been swallowed up in victory."

Royal Mindset

On a daily basis, worldly life swirls around us. Even though we become citizens of the Kingdom of God the moment we place our faith in Jesus as our Savior and Lord, we remain living on this planet until He calls us home through our passing, or until He returns for us at the end of this age. As we go about our daily routines we need to keep our eyes firmly focused on the One who is ultimately in charge, the One who has given us a hope and future, and the promise of everlasting life. We're encouraged to not allow ourselves to become overwhelmed by the things we face, but overcome anything by focusing on Jesus and His perspective on everything. God is so much bigger than whatever we encounter—as He sits on His throne in Heaven, the earth is His mere footstool. Focus on the eternal hope we have, while addressing the temporary. Compared to the boundless glory that awaits us, our troubles suddenly seem small and momentary. We may not understand everything now, but someday Jesus will make it all clear—until then ask God to help you keep a royal mindset.

2 Corinthians 4:16-18, "Therefore we do not lose heart. Though outwardly we are wasting away, yet inwardly we are being renewed day by day. [17] For our light and momentary troubles are achieving for us an eternal glory that far outweighs them all. [18] So we fix our eyes not on what is seen, but on what is unseen, since what is seen is temporary, but what is unseen is eternal."

Royal Servants

As with most things in the Kingdom of God, the idea of *who is greatest* is another which is flipped upside-down in contrast to what the world says. With Jesus as our supreme example, being ruler over all, having every reason to lord His position over everyone's head, He took the attitude of a servant. He laid down His place of honor to serve us. Jesus washed His disciple's feet; Jesus died on the cross for our sake. As His followers, our attitude is to be the same. As citizens in the Kingdom of God we aren't supposed to stand in a place of criticism and judgment over others, we are meant to stand in a place of servanthood, loving people into the Kingdom with open arms, as an extension of Jesus.

Luke 22:24-27, "A dispute also arose among them as to which of them was considered to be greatest. ²⁵ Jesus said to them, 'The kings of the Gentiles lord it over them; and those who exercise authority over them call themselves Benefactors. ²⁶ But you are not to be like that. Instead, the greatest among you should be like the youngest, and the one who rules like the one who serves. ²⁷ For who is greater, the one who is at the table or the one who serves? Is it not the one who is at the table? But I am among you as one who serves.'"

Royal Ambassadors

Along with the royal privileges *a daughter of the King* receives, she is also required to exercise her royal duties. Although she is granted eternal security in the Kingdom of her Father, she doesn't get to sit around with her head in the clouds; she has responsibilities to tend to. We are that daughter—through Jesus Christ, God has reconciled us to Himself and calls us His beloved child. As a valued member of His family, God entrusts to us His message of love and salvation, not to keep for ourselves but to share with others who are lost, lonely, weak, hurting, and scared. We have been given the greatest honor of all, representing Jesus to the world, through our words and actions. We have been entrusted with the task of sharing the Gospel, and inviting others to be reconciled to God through Jesus, and into His Kingdom as well. We are ambassadors of Christ Himself, as if God were making His appeal to others through us. People need to hear about Jesus in order to believe. We are sent to share the message and be the *"beautiful feet that bring good news."*

Romans 10:13-15, "'for, 'Everyone who calls on the name of the Lord will be saved.' 14 How, then, can they call on the one they have not believed in? And how can they believe in the one of whom they have not heard? And how can they hear without someone preaching to them? 15 And how can anyone preach unless they are sent? As it is written: 'How beautiful are the feet of those who bring good news!'"

In Closing

My dear *daughter of the King*, precious child of God, let me leave you with some final encouragements:

Continually bask in the love that God has for you. He calls you His beloved and promises to never leave your side.

Continually seek God and His Kingdom first. Let everything else in life follow along after these. Pursue Him wholeheartedly and everything else will make more sense.

Continually pray and give thanks and praise to His Name. God is the source of everything good and all that you'll ever need.

Continually hold onto hope for today and tomorrow. Jesus holds both in His competent hands.

Continually rejoice, for your name is written in Heaven. When Jesus returns and opens His Book, your name will be highlighted as a welcome guest of honor.

Continually reflect on your knowledge of The Almighty God and your relationship to Him. Your identity is built on nothing less.

I thank you for joining me on this confidence quest. I pray that the previous pages have revealed and confirmed just how precious God thinks you are. The more time you spend with Him in prayer and His Word, the more confident you'll continue to grow. Dear sister-in-Christ, though we may never meet, we're on this journey together.

Sending my love and blessings,

Tracy

So Grateful

To Russell, Camden, and Christian—you hold my heart in your hands.

To Russell, who has stood by me all these years. Thank you for loving me despite myself. You represent Jesus well. Thank you for partnering with me in the raising of our precious family. Thank you for providing and allowing me the opportunity to serve the Lord and His ladies—in this way you serve Him too. Thank you for your patience during times of writing. I hope your eggs were hot and your coffee was cold.

To Camden, for your encouragement and lovely book covers. Thank you for phone calls that keep me going between visits, when I can give you a big hug.

To Christian, for correcting my obsession with commas. Thank you for not growing too old to hang out with your Mom. I treasure our times together.

To Melanie, for taking the time to refine my words, grammar, and punctuation, and also confirm that I'm making sense. And most definitely for being my dear friend.

To Kimbra, for your friendship, your prayers, and for modeling faith. Time spent with you is a breath of fresh air.

Getting to Know the Author

First and foremost, I am a woman who loves the Lord with all her heart. I am married to a wonderful man, and I'm a mother of two young men (who used to be small). I am a daughter, a sister, a friend, a neighbor. I have a dog, I enjoy taking walks outside, and I like chips and salsa. I'm involved in the women's ministry at my local church in Westlake Village, California. I enjoy speaking at Teen Challenge International, and other various women's events. I have a passion for helping women deepen their relationship with Jesus and discover their identity as a child of God through the study of His Word. Although you and I may have different likes or dislikes, relationships or roles, I'm sure many of my life stories can be related to whatever you have going on. I truly thank you for joining me on this journey and hope that you find encouragement as we walk together with the Lord.

Connect with me on Facebook at: facebook.com/tracyhillauthor

Follow my blog at: tracy-considerthelilies.blogspot.com

Titles available in stores and online at <u>Amazon.com</u>:

A Daughter of the King: Gaining Confidence as a Child of God
(A Bible Study)

Excerpt: God's desire is for you to discover the confidence and rich blessings of your true identity which are found in Jesus Christ. The enemy wants you to believe otherwise, so you are going to learn to fight off the lies of insecurity with solid Truth. You are meant to live in confidence and victory as a Daughter of the King. You are royalty.

Lilies and Lemonade: Joy-Filled Devotions

Excerpt: *Lilies and Lemonade* represents two philosophies which hold the key to optimistic living. A joy-filled perspective is available to us when we look at life with the proper Jesus-filled mindset.

Promise and Possibilities: Hope-Filled Devotions

Excerpt: You will glimpse the promise that life holds and the possibility of all that can be when you place your hope in Jesus. He's truly the One who holds the key.

Confidence and Crowns: Devotions for A Daughter of the King

Excerpt: The devotions, stories, and Scripture you'll encounter, are all intended to point you to the reality of who you are in God's eyes. My prayer is that you come away inspired, that you stand a little taller, hold your head a little higher, walk with a new spring in your step, and begin to face life head-on, armed with the knowledge of your true identity. It's time to put aside your doubts and insecurities and live a life of confidence.

Made in the USA
San Bernardino, CA
21 November 2018